# Simple Publicity

How to do your own public
relations to boost sales,
awareness and credibility fast...
without spending a lot of money!

To ██████,

Thank you for all
your kindness!

♡ Melanie

Simple Publicity

How to do your own public relations to boost sales, awareness and credibility fast...
without spending a lot of money!

By Melanie Rembrandt

Printed in the United States of America

The author and publisher have made every effort to ensure the accuracy of the
information contained in this book but assume no responsibility for actions taken as a
result of the content. If you see errors, please contact us at www.1winpress.com.

Copyright © 2010
Melanie Rembrandt
1Win Press™
www.1winpress.com

ISBN: 0982695055
EAN-13: 9780982695050
LCCN: 2010904055

# Simple Publicity

How to do your own public relations to boost sales, awareness and credibility fast... without spending a lot of money!

By Melanie Rembrandt

1Win Press™ · Los Angeles, CA

# Buzz About This Book

"If you are starting a business and want to build credibility and bring in new sales fast using the 'power of publicity,' check out this book.

In a matter of hours, you'll know how to contact the media to get press coverage, give great interviews, create press-releases and media kits, and much more!"

*Cynthia Good, CEO, Editor PINK®*

"Entrepreneurs are challenged with time, energy and focus. They are busy running their businesses, and they need help with their PR and SEO efforts and guidance on how to do it efficiently.

Finally, here's a simple guide on how to do your own publicity! Melanie Rembrandt has condensed her extensive experience and success in the field of public relations into an easy, step-by-step approach anyone can follow."

*David Wolf, SmallBiz America Network™*

"I love books with action plans. Rembrandt's book is full of them! She shares practical steps and actions that you can take even without a big, fancy budget.

Loved all the little 'in-between' stuff that nobody else writes about but that's so critical to succeeding in any PR effort. Get Rembrandt's book, and get known!"

*Rich Sloan, StartupNation® Co-founder and Chief Startupologist*

"The information in this book helped me get noticed by key media-members, increase my income and catapult my career success!

Veteran publicist and SEO copywriter Melanie Rembrandt reveals her PR secrets in a simple format that's affordable and easy-to-read. If you want to make more money and take your business to the next level, buy this book."

*Tara-Nicholle Nelson, Esq., REThink Real Estate Founder and Chief Visionary and spokesperson for Trulia®*

# Contents

## Chapter 5 – What Are You Going To Provide?     51

*To Chris, My Family, Kathleen, and Gail –*

*Thank you for being my support network through thick and thin.
I'm blessed to have you in my life.*

# Introduction

As a new business owner or entrepreneur, you know you need public relations, but you may be overwhelmed by all of the information that is available.

In this book, I hope to make it as easy as possible for you to learn about the nuts and bolts of publicity – and how you can use it to your advantage to help increase sales, awareness and credibility fast.

## WHAT IS PUBLIC RELATIONS?

To start, Public Relations, or "PR," refers to any communication you have with people regarding your business. This includes the conversations you have with internal, team members and outside sources such as: customers, media-members, investors, vendors, sponsors, and partners.

Public-relations activities usually center around communications with media-members. This is because when the right message about your business is told via a television, radio, print, or online story, you can reach thousands of potential customers and increase sales cost-effectively.

More important, when outside parties talk about your products and services, you create third-party credibility that cannot be purchased through advertising. This word-of-mouth buzz and increased awareness can help catapult your business to super success. That's why they call it the "power of PR."

And as an entrepreneur, there are many advantages to using PR that are really exciting. In fact, after working with numerous, small businesses for many years, I've found that there are four major myths about having a successful, public-relations program.

## THE 4 PR MYTHS — BUSTED!

### PR Myth #1 - You Need a Lot of Money!

No, you don't! Halleluiah! Just what you wanted to hear! Yes, it is simply not true that you need a lot of money to pursue public-relations efforts. It really just takes time and effort.

In fact, as a new entrepreneur, you may lose a lot of money and sleep by spending big bucks on a large, public-relations agency. I've talked to many business owners who were completely frustrated at the process. After spending thousands of dollars, they received minimal attention and press mentions.

Why? Many large, PR agencies will be interested in having you as a client and taking your retainer fees. But then, as one of their smaller accounts, you may not get the attention you deserve.

This doesn't happen all the time, but a recent college-graduate or intern may handle your account. Then, you may not see the results of working with a well-known agency. And by the time you realize this, your complete, PR budget can disappear!

## PR Myth #2 - You Must Hire a Publicist!

If you are just starting out and don't have the money to hire a publicist, you can get some fantastic press coverage on your own. But you need to be willing to take the time to make it happen. This book aims to help you do just that.

After creating a plan, conducting the appropriate research and taking action, it is possible to get targeted media venues to spread the word about your business.

And this refers to more than just the local press. You can book interviews with nationally-syndicated television and radio programs. You can appear on the cover of *The New York Times, Fortune* and *The Wall Street Journal*, talk to "Oprah" and the morning radio-show-host, chat on a popular blog, and be on any other media venue you go after!

It's just a matter of researching in advance and taking action.

## PR Myth #3 - You Can't Get Good Press Because You Don't Own a Big Business!

Wrong! It's time to stop the limitations and think big. As a small business owner, you actually have an advantage over big business in obtaining good press. Why? Here are five good reasons:

### 1. Only you have the passion.

Your business is your "baby" and you have more passion about it than anyone else on the planet. And only you can convey this passion as you communicate to the media and potential customers and partners.

Large businesses have comprehensive, communications-departments to talk about their news and events to the media. And often, the strong, passionate feelings about the business can weaken as growth and financial priorities take precedence.

Think how nice it is for a reporter to talk to a person who is truly passionate and optimistic about what he or she does in today's onslaught of negativity and bad news?

## 2. You have a unique story to tell.

Most people have not heard about your business, and reporters love this. It gives them the opportunity to be the first to cover a new, fresh story that has not been told before.

Plus, only you can share the specific details about how you created and pursued your business idea to make it a reality.

## 3. You can move fast without an extended, approval process.

With larger companies, there are usually more people, departments and communication channels to go through in order to obtain approval on various advertising and publicity messages. This takes extra time.

As a small business owner, you have the advantage of calling the shots and making decisions quickly. This enables you to get appropriate information to the media fast.

Plus, it will be much easier for reporters to reach you, the owner and leader of the business. Without the hassle of dealing with a corporate hierarchy, they can get the inside information they need from you, write a great story and meet their tight deadlines.

## 4. You can build personal, media relationships.

Larger organizations have teams of leaders in various departments who talk to the press, depending on who is available. Since you will be handling all of the interviews, you can create personal relationships directly with media-members.

By talking to various reporters, you can offer your expertise as a resource for future articles and keep in touch with breaking news-stories.

If you provide credible, newsworthy information on a regular basis, and reporters are able to get in touch with you quickly, you'll establish valuable relationships that can turn into major, media-mentions in the future.

## 5. You can control your messaging.

Since you'll be handling all of the media interviews, you can control what is said, how you sell your products and services, the tone/style, and the timing of your important messaging.

Rather than checking with a legal team or communications department to hone a specific message, you can respond to media-members, and answer interviews questions quickly and accurately.

Reporters know that they can get in touch with you, confirm story facts and move quickly without having to go through other departments. It's a win-win situation for you and media-members.

## PR Myth Buster #4 – Press Releases Are All You Need.

Most entrepreneurs immediately think of sending out a press release when they think of public relations.

*But press releases are not always the answer.*

In fact, by sending out a blanket press-release to a list of thousands of media-members, you can actually hurt your reputation with the media!

Today's media-relations practices involve targeted pitching where the right story angle is developed and communicated to specific reporters, producers and editors at the right time.

A press release can help customers find your business online via the search engines, get newsworthy information out to the right people and help you accomplish other, unique business goals. But it is not usually the answer for obtaining large numbers of media quotes or press clippings.

Instead, think of a press release as a relationship-builder. Use it to remind important customers, partners, investors, employees, sponsors, and certain media-members that you have current news, products and services and that your business is up-to-date and growing.

In fact, if you have a tight budget and schedule, I suggest spending the majority of your publicity time talking to targeted reporters via phone or in person rather than sending out a press release to the masses.

This way, you can share your passion and introduce yourself to appropriate, media-members directly. And this is usually much more beneficial than writing a press release and simply distributing it to a blanketed list of hundreds of media venues.

Whether or not these myths come as a surprise to you or not, public-relations does not need to be a mystery. You can use it to your advantage to help your business boost sales, awareness and credibility fast... so let's get started!

# CHAPTER 1

# WHAT'S YOUR GOAL?

Why set goals? Before you start your public-relations activities, it's important to decide exactly what you want to accomplish.

After all, you don't want to spend a lot of time and effort on PR activities just because you heard it was necessary to have publicity as a new entrepreneur.

And if you don't know what you want to accomplish, how are you going to get there? It's impossible to get from "Point A" to "Point B" if you don't know where "Point B" is!

There needs to be some kind of foundation to actually avoid wasting time, money and effort. And I'm sure you've heard the importance of setting goals and writing them down:

"Setting goals is the first step in turning the invisible into the visible." *Tony Robbins*

"If you want to be happy, set a goal that commands your thoughts, liberates your energy and inspires your hopes." *Andrew Carnegie*

"The tragedy of life doesn't lie in not reaching your goal. The tragedy lies in having no goal to reach."
*Benjamin E. Mays*

"Goals are not only absolutely necessary to motivate us. They are essential to really keep us alive." *Robert H. Schuller*

"You have to know what you want to get." *Gertrude Stein*

"My philosophy of life is that if we make up our mind what we are going to make of our lives, then work hard toward that goal, we never lose - somehow we win out."
*Ronald Reagan*

"Man is a goal seeking animal. His life only has meaning if he is reaching out and striving for his goals." *Aristotle*

## WHAT ARE YOUR GOALS?

This advice may be redundant, but goals can help you get in the right mindset to actually accomplish your dreams. With this in mind, do you know what your PR goals are?

To get started, review your business plan and decide what is really important. Maybe you want to be rich, improve the environment and help those who are less fortunate, or just have more free time to yourself.

Think about the key activities that will make you truly successful. If you could do anything, and it was impossible to fail, what would you like to accomplish now and in five years?

Write down your dreams for your business (no matter how big or small) here:

**Goal This Year:**

_____

_____

_____

**Goal in Five Years:**

_____

_____

_____

**Goal in Ten Years:**

_____

_____

_____

Picture achieving each of these goals in your mind. You can make them a reality. It's a matter of planning and taking action.

## PR ACTIVITIES VS. RESULTS

Now that you know what you want to accomplish, take a realistic look at how you think your publicity efforts will help you reach your goals. From your efforts, do you hope to increase sales, find new customers, build credibility, or just make people aware that you are open for business?

After all, a guest appearance on a major, television program may be great for your ego. But if your main goal is to increase sales, and your target audience doesn't watch that program, you won't reach your goal via this publicity effort.

To get organized, look at your overall, business aspirations, and think about the public-relations results that will help you achieve these goals.

For example, do you want to be on the cover of *Entrepreneur Magazine,* talk to "Oprah," have an interview on a local radio station, be featured in specific, industry publications, etc.?

## What's Your Brand?

In addition to your personal publicity-goals, you also need to consider the brand-image you want to create, or what people think about your business.

For example, if you interviewed your customers right now, what would they have to say about your business?

Your answer will determine the status of your brand and give hints as to the kind of public-relations efforts you'll need to make an impact on target audiences.

And if you don't like the responses, or just want to create a new brand-image, this will be an important aspect of your PR efforts.

## An Easy Way to Start

To help you get a better understanding of what your business really needs to succeed, take a look at these questions.

Your responses will help you focus on public relations efforts that will help you achieve your goals faster. And by actually writing down your answers, you will be more focused and one step closer to achieving success.

1. When people hear the name of your company, what do you want them to think about?

_____

_____

_____

_____

_____

2. What can you do to help your audiences think about your company in this way?

_____

_____

_____

_____

_____

3. Why are your products and services unique? Why should a customer buy from you rather than the competition? List as many attributes as possible.

_____

_____

_____

_____

_____

4. **What are key benefits of your products and services? What does the customer receive?**

_____

_____

_____

_____

_____

5. **Do you have some happy customers who would be willing to share their success stories? List a few here.**

_____

_____

_____

_____

_____

6. **What are the most important things about your business that you want media-members to talk about?**

_____

_____

_____

_____

_____

7. **What do you specifically hope to accomplish through your public-relations efforts?**

_____

_____

_____

_____

_____

Now, review your responses. Think about what you need to do to activate your publicity efforts right now. Write your PR goals down for this year here:

**PR Goals This Year:**

_____

_____

_____

_____

Later on, you can review this information to see if you are on track and if changes need to be made. Remember, it's important to focus on the final results you want to achieve and how specific, PR efforts will affect these outcomes.

## PR Time and Budget

There is no reason not to dream big and have goals of being on national, television programs and radio shows and quoted in major, media-venues.

However, these efforts cost valuable time. With this in mind, you'll want to think about how much of your schedule can be devoted to public-relations activities.

*What will it take to accomplish your publicity goals in relation to your overall, business goals?*

Once you know what you want to accomplish, you'll have a better understanding of how your publicity efforts fit into your overall, business goals. You can do your own PR, but if you have the funds, it may be well worth the money to create a PR budget.

This way, you can seek the help of an experienced, public-relations expert, and spend your time focusing on your expertise and core business essentials.

# CHAPTER 2

# Wнат's Your Plan?

Once you have a good understanding of what you want to accomplish with public relations, you'll want to get organized and create an action-plan. This "PR Plan" will spell out all of the activities, events and timelines necessary to meet your goals.

But please don't feel overwhelmed. Depending on your specific needs and timeframe, your PR Plan can be short and sweet with just basic information about activities and scheduling. Or, it can include detailed data about competitors, media-members, your industry, company strengths and weaknesses, mission statements, economic forecasts, potential customers, budgets, goals, and more.

The length doesn't matter. What's important is that you include the specific, PR activities (and schedule for these efforts) that you need to reach your goals.

You can create an outline, write down tasks in a calendar or create a document detailing your activities – whatever works best for you and your business. But as you write your PR Plan, there are several, key concepts you'll want to include:

## PUBLICIZE BENEFITS VS. FEATURES.

*Always focus on benefits rather than features.*

As an entrepreneur, you are probably very passionate about your products and services. And you probably can't wait to talk about all of the details, background and technology behind your new business.

This is great information for credibility purposes, *but it is not necessarily newsworthy.*

As you create your action plan (and pursue all business and PR activities for that matter), always think about your audience first.

Why will media-members, customers, potential partners, and others care about what you have to say?

What will your products and services do for them?

### *Rather than discuss detailed features, focus on benefits.*

But what is the difference between a benefit and a feature?

This may seem rudimentary, but it's important. Benefits relate to what the feature does or how it makes you feel. For example, a pencil has an eraser. It is bright yellow and provides a way to write with lead that you sharpen frequently. These are all features of the pencil.

On the contrary, some of the benefits of the pencil are that it allows you to:

- Erase mistakes quickly;

- Save money over purchasing more expensive writing utensils;

- Reduce stress knowing that if you lose the pencil you can easily replace it; and

- Save time writing underwater, upside down or anywhere you need to make a note.

This may be a very simple concept, but it is easy to forget in business communications and media relations. Therefore, the next time you sit down to write, make the extra effort to talk about the benefits each of your products or services offers. What will your customers want to know about? Constantly ask yourself:

*"What's in it for them?"*

By remembering this one, simple point, your pitches and content will be much more interesting and newsworthy. You'll also see better results, and save a lot of extra time and effort in the process.

## CHOOSE TARGETED, MEDIA VENUES.

Even if you are a small-business owner, there is no reason to think small when it comes to media venues. While it's great to get some interview experience at the local level, *do not limit yourself.*

As mentioned earlier, media-members want unique, fresh stories. And you have exactly what they are looking for!

With this in mind, think of the top ten media-venues you would love to have talk about your business. Make a list of all the television programs, radio shows, online media, and print publications you want to approach. And remember, the sky's the limit.

*Think BIG, and you'll be more likely to garner more media attention with better results.*

Also, don't forget to think about the media-venues that your potential customers watch, listen to and read. There are many lesser-known niche publications, blogs and other venues that need regular content and news.

These venues may not seem like huge opportunities to you, but they can help you build credibility and reach your target audience fast.

## PROMOTE THE RIGHT MESSAGE.

What kind of media buzz do you want to build? If you can have reporters write about your business, what do you want them to say?

Think about the unique aspects of what you have to offer and what is newsworthy. Remember to focus on the benefits you provide to others. People want to know what's in it for them... not about all of the specific features you have to offer.

Write down all of the key concepts that you think are unique about your business and why a customer should buy from you rather than the competition. To start, answer these questions:

*What are the top three concepts about your business that you want publicized?*

1. _____

_____

_____

_____

2. _____

_____

_____

_____

3. _____

_____

_____

_____

*What are three, newsworthy items about your business that you can talk about right now?*

1. _____

_____

_____

_____

2. _____

_____

_____

_____

3. _____

   _____

   _____

   _____

Now, you'll use these basic ideas to create story angles that reporters will be interested in potentially pursuing.

Review your responses and ask yourself if a reporter will care about these items. If not, you need to conduct more research and really think about what your business has to offer that is newsworthy. And with this in mind...

## WHAT IS NEWSWORTHY?

If you are like me, you are probably bombarded with information on the latest Web technology, networking, videos, RSS feeds, social media, and more on a daily basis. In additional to traditional publicity activities, all of this information can make your head spin.

*But don't worry! When it comes right down to it, all you need to do is focus on one thing... your unique, story angle.*

If you have newsworthy and interesting information that is relevant to a specific, media venue at the right time, you will get press coverage.

This is a simple concept, and best of all, it only costs you research-time. After all, if you want to reach specific objectives, it's very important to look at the best way to get your news promoted, and figure out who will be interested in what you have to say.

Once you study your targeted media-venues and have a unique story angle for each, you'll have a much better understanding of the PR opportunities that will work best for your specific situation and budget. This planning and research process will help you save time, money and frustration. Plus, it will ensure that you focus on the right activities to accomplish your goals.

## Need Help Finding Newsworthy Angles?

Now, if you are having difficulty coming up with newsworthy ideas, think about these questions:

- What part of your business is related to a current news story, holiday or industry event?

- Do you have a strong opinion about a current headline?

- What kind of challenges/personal hardships did you go through to create your business?

- Can you provide tips and advice to others?

- What are the unique benefits of your products and services that no one else offers?

- Will one of your customers share their "before-and-after" story?

- Are you working with a particular charity or supporting some kind of community effort?

You can also find newsworthy ideas in other ways. For example:

- Track competitor information to discover what they are promoting;

- Study industry trends and news;

- Review all of the benefits you have to offer;

- Create new benefits for your products and services pertinent to your customers' needs; and

- Ask others what they think is newsworthy about your business and why your products and services are different.

By being aware of industry news and conducting the appropriate research on a regular basis, you will discover some interesting story ideas and newsworthy-information unique to your business.

## PROMOTE VIA NETWORKING.

Another important concept to include in your PR Plan is networking. As an entrepreneur, it's essential to promote your business on a regular basis. By meeting the right people and establishing your credibility with pertinent, online communities, local organizations and national, industry-related groups, you'll help to increase sales and awareness.

And if you are a shy person, and the thought of getting out and mingling with complete strangers terrifies you, don't worry. Here are a few, quick tips.

### Start small and work your way up.

Get involved with online forums and communities where your customers hang out. Then, when you feel more comfortable talking about your business, attend a local event with a friend or co-worker.

But before you go, think about how you will present yourself, what you will talk about and the image you want to create. You can start a conversation by simply introducing yourself, commenting on a particular food-item at the event or giving a compliment.

And don't worry about carrying the conversation. The best way to network is to listen to what others have to say. Ask about their interests and hobbies, and talk about their business needs. Just by being yourself and a good listener, you'll start to create relationships and meet people with varied backgrounds.

Be sure to exchange business cards with the people you meet. And when you get a private moment, jot down a few notes regarding your conversations on the back of each card. This will help you remember people in the future and conduct the appropriate follow-up.

## Learn about others.

Instead of thinking of a networking-event as a place to sell your products and services, think of it as a place to learn about new people and what is important to them.

By focusing on the needs of others without having a sales agenda, you will be less nervous and have a better conversation. Plus, you may get some great ideas that will help you grow your business, discover new resources and find out more about your target audience.

As a small business owner, it's important to network and have good, speaking skills. And if these are not your biggest strengths, consider taking a communication class or working with a coach. Even if you are not shy, make an effort to hone your communication-skills and meet new people on a regular basis to help expand your business network.

## ATTEND EVENTS THAT MATTER.

Since networking is a basic part of business success, it's important to think about where your networking skills will pay off the most. On your PR Plan, make a list of all the pertinent local, national and industry-related events that are important for your business.

To simplify this process, ask yourself these questions:

- Where will you meet the most influential people to help you reach your business goals?

_____

_____

_____

- Where do members of your target audience hang out?

_____

_____

_____

- What do you want to accomplish at each of these events?

_____

_____

_____

- How will you get involved at this event? Will you give a presentation? Sell products? Have a booth?

_____

_____

_____

- When are these events happening, and what are the appropriate deadlines you need to be aware of?

_____

_____

_____

- What kind of a budget do you have for event-participation this year?

_____

_____

_____

- Why are these event activities worth it?

_____

_____

_____

These questions will help you decide which events (presentations, tradeshows, conventions, organizational meetings, etc.) are important.

And it's always wise to plan events in advance. Not only do deadlines come up quickly, but you can save a lot of time and money by making the appropriate preparations.

With this in mind, try to review your event-participation at the beginning of each year. It may help to create a separate, smaller PR-plan for each event.

For example, in your "Event PR Plan," you can write down exactly what you want to accomplish at each event, who will be involved, how much it will cost, and what tasks need to be accomplished in order to reach your event goals. You'll also want to include your messaging, news-announcements, media-contacts, timing, and all other details related to the event.

When each event is finished, measure your results so that you can make the appropriate changes for future participation and other, upcoming events.

## ARE EVENTS REALLY WORTH IT?

Now, with everything you have going on as a small business owner, event-participation may be the last thing on your priority list. However, it can be well worth the effort.

For example, let's say your competitor gives a presentation at a local Chamber of Commerce meeting. He promotes the presentation in advance and then provides valuable information to his target audience (a.k.a. your potential customers). It is a newsworthy event so media-members attend and take his photo.

While you missed out on the opportunity, your competitor meets new customers and establishes credibility. Plus, he creates a relationship with a local business reporter for future stories and is quoted as a credible, industry expert in the newspaper the next day.

Your competitor then uses this media-clip on his Web site and in his marketing materials to attract new customers, more speaking opportunities and press coverage.

The same goes for tradeshows, conventions and other industry events. With advanced planning, event-participation is an excellent way to gain new customers and media coverage quickly without spending a lot of money. Try to make it a priority in your PR Plan.

## TEAM UP WITH BIG ORGANIZATIONS.

Participating in events is important, but one of the great ways to generate press cost-effectively is to create your own event and partner with a well-known company, organization or charity.

This not only allows you to share the time, effort and budget involved, but you can also increase your chances of acquiring more media-attention and reaching a larger audience of potential, new customers.

To start, conduct some research to see which organizations cater to your audience and have similar beliefs. Find out if these potential partners have participated in local and national events in the past, who was involved and what the final results entailed.

Make a list of all potential possibilities here. And there is no reason to think small. Start with people you know and local organizations. Then, write down all of your dream-partnerships.

- _____
- _____
- _____
- _____

- _____
- _____

Now, develop specific, event ideas for each potential partner. You'll want to list the benefits for that partner, potential costs, time involved, and the people it will take to accomplish event goals. Try to create an enticing offer for your partner and think...

### *"What's in it for them?"*

This way, the event will be successful for both of you and build positive word-of-mouth months after the event occurs.

## Creative Event-Ideas

And if you need some help thinking of a creative event, try these suggestions:

- Check the calendar for upcoming holidays, special days and local activities that happen each year.

- Review local charities to see how your specific products and services can help them succeed.

- Prepare a special presentation for a specific audience and provide door prizes.

- Create a unique, online or live competition/prize.

- Develop a special, sporting activity specific to your audience.

- Get involved with an upcoming performance, book-signing or concert popular with your target market.

- Think of things you can give away and then develop a specific event with a potential partner.

These are just a few thoughts. Be creative! Just keep in mind that the best events that garner the most media attention focus on helping others. Plus, you'll spend your time and effort on a worthwhile cause while building credibility and awareness.

Once you have some ideas in mind, contact the person at each organization who handles partnerships and/or events. Then, pitch your idea and "sell" the benefits for their organization first.

And with events, remember that you can always start with little or no budget, outsource specifics and ask for donations. Then, as your budget and audience grows, you'll be able to attract larger partners and sponsors.

## USE CONTENT TO BUILD BUZZ.

One of the best ways to increase awareness is through content. By writing various forms of copy yourself, or hiring a ghostwriter, you can get some great media placements and build credibility cost-effectively.

Here are a few forms of content to add to your overall, PR Plan on a regular basis:

### Web Site Copy

Do you have a marketing Web site? If not, you need one... no matter what kind of business you have.

Today, all businesses need a Web site in order to show credibility and stay ahead of the competition. Plus, an online presence offers a great way to communicate with current and potential customers, and the press, at any time.

Now, there are many quick and easy ways to get a Web site up and running. For help, check with your peers for recommendations, and conduct research online for a Web site service that meets your specific needs and budget.

And if you have a Web site, does it focus on benefits rather than features? Take a close look at your online copy, and see if it provides your target audience-members with the information they need.

- Are you helping site visitors solve a problem quickly?

- Why should they use your products and services over the competition?

- Do all of the links work, and is the site current and professional?

To get a better idea of the message your current Web site conveys, have outsiders read the copy, and get their opinions. If you have the funds, hire a search engine optimization (SEO) copywriter to write your Web page content for you. Although this may seem like an added expense, it is worth it in the end. You'll have a professional and current Web site that works without wasting your time or effort.

Plus, an experienced SEO copywriter will include "copy that sells" and analytics. This way, potential customers will actually be able to find your business via the search engines (like Google™ and Yahoo!™). You'll be able to track visits and make changes accordingly.

And once your updated site goes live, be sure to add new copy on a regular basis, check for errors and review analytics. This way, you'll give customers what they want and start building awareness online.

## Original Articles

You can build credibility and awareness fast by writing your own articles and having them posted on targeted, Web sites or in key media-publications. Working with tight budgets, many media-venues are looking for "free" content and expert contributors. Plus, this is a great way to build buzz about your expertise and control your messaging while obtaining some good publicity.

And if you aren't a writer, look for a ghostwriter to assist you. Check online and at local schools for help. There are many freelance writers and college students looking for project-based work. This can save you a lot of time and effort in the long run.

To start your writing efforts, conduct research, and decide which media venues you want to pursue. Look at editorial calendars for each (this is a list of upcoming topics for advertisers). Then, figure out what kind of articles you can provide pertinent to these topics.

Perhaps you can offer tips, a case study, survey results, or other, helpful information?

Once you have some good, topic ideas, check each venue for specific "writer guidelines" with requirements for tone, style and length. Then, contact the pertinent editors to see if they are interested in having you write an original article about your chosen topics or if they have another story-idea for you to write.

You can also write an article and then send it to the appropriate person at the publication. But if they are not interested, you'll have to send it to another publication until you find someone willing to publish it "as is."

Whenever possible, pitch your story-idea to the appropriate person, and try to secure a placement *prior* to writing the article. This will save time and help you focus your writing efforts on the publications you want to reach.

## Tip Sheets

Reporters love quick and unique tips that are easy to read and interesting to their audience. You can take advantage of this opportunity by developing "Top 10 Lists" (ex. "Top 10 Things to Watch Out For When Buying Life Insurance," "Top 7 Ways to Avoid Losing Money on Plumbing Services, etc.). You can also use bullet-points on helpful ways for your customers to fix simple problems fast (ex. "How to Fix Sink Back-Up in 3 Easy Steps," "How to Find the Right Hair Stylist for Your Hair," etc.).

You can then send these directly to media-members, use them in press releases, post them on your Web site, or send them directly to customers via a newsletter. They also make great sidebars in your original articles.

## Case Studies

A case study is basically a detailed, "before-and-after" story that offers credibility for your products and services. If you have some customers willing to give their testimonials, you'll want to use this information to your advantage.

To create a case study, interview your clients and try to get specific details on how your business has helped them succeed. If they can provide sales-growth increases, percentages in time and money saved since working with you, why they chose your services, and other key numbers, this will add to the credibility of your case study.

When you have this information, simply tell what your customer does, how they used your business and how your products and services made a significant difference to their bottom-line and solved their specific problem(s). For sample case-studies, tip sheets, articles, and more, check out those from your competitors and businesses you admire. Also conduct searches online for samples related to your specific industry.

Once you have your case study (or tip sheet), you can pitch it to a specific media venue as an "exclusive" before publishing the data anywhere else. An "exclusive," is a story that you promise a reporter first before sharing the information with any other media-member.

Many reporters will be interested in these "personal stories of success" that provide specific numbers and proof of growth. Plus, if you get your case study published by a targeted media-venue, this will significantly increase your credibility.

But be careful.

***If you promise an exclusive story to a reporter, be sure that this reporter gets the exclusive.***

Do not share the information with others until that reporter's story is published. Otherwise, you could be blacklisted by this reporter and have a difficult time getting coverage in this media venue again. Even worse, a reporter may write a negative story about you and your business that can spread across your industry fast.

In addition, reporters talk to one another within the media community, and you may be banned from more than just one venue if you break the "exclusive story" rules or lack professionalism.

With this in mind, when you hear about unethical business practices in the PR and advertising world, think about how you would like to be treated, and act accordingly. After all, you do not want your business dreams crushed by extensive, bad publicity.

By building a reputation as a reliable and honest resource that is easy-to-do-business-with, you will build credibility that can result in more media-placements that produce the results you want.

And if you are not able to secure a media placement by pitching your case study as an exclusive, be sure to promote it accordingly. You can create a press release about the results, and work with your customer on joint publicity-efforts to save time and money.

Most importantly, you can post the case study on your Web site and use it in your marketing efforts to provide proof and credibility to potential new customers.

## White Papers

If you have a lot of information to share with potential customers about a specific, technology-process, invention, detailed case-study, or other extensive data, you'll want to develop a white paper.

Basically, these are reports or articles that describe specifics about your products and/or services in great detail. For example, if you are selling an expensive product or service, white papers can help answer customer-questions, provide credibility and give the specifics necessary to close a sale.

And again, if you need samples, check the sites of businesses you admire and those of your competitors. Also, conduct online searches for white papers in your industry.

## Social Media

Social media is basically a way to communicate with people so they can interact with you online. And there are many ways to use social media.

But before adding it to your PR Plan and simply "jumping on the bandwagon," think about your target-audience.

- Do they use social media venues?

- Is it worth it for you to take the time and energy to keep your social-media communications current?

With this in mind, here are some ways to use social media in your PR efforts:

## Blogs

Short for "Web log," blogs are online diaries that can be updated in real-time. Basically, a person can create a blog online about any topic and write about it. The best blogs contain links to resources, current insights and valuable information about a specific topic.

Blogs are a great way to share updated information with your target audience and generate awareness on the Web. Best of all, you can use one of the free services available like Blogger™, www.blogger.com and WordPress.com™, www.wordpress.com, to easily create your blog in a matter of minutes.

To start, review blogs at various companies you admire, and figure out the topic you want to write about and the purpose of your blog.

- Do you want to write about a problem in your industry and provide your insights on how to fix it?

- Maybe you want to give some resources and links for people to find information?

- Perhaps, you want to focus on how your business is related to a current, news-item or industry-trend?

Once you know what you want to write about, create a blog title, set a writing schedule or editorial calendar, and start writing.

If you don't feel comfortable writing on the World Wide Web for all to see, find a co-worker or ghostwriter to write the blog for you. It can be highly beneficial to hire a blog copywriter because that person can add SEO keywords so that your entries get "picked up" by the search engines and attract more visitors.

And don't forget to include a section for comments at the end of your blog. This way, customers can offer their feedback, and you can respond quickly. Not only will this help you build relationships with your customers and see what they really want, but you'll also be aware of small issues and have the opportunity to stop them from progressing into major problems. In addition, media-members may write about your blog and give you some free publicity.

Blogs are great communication tools, but keep this in mind:

*The key factor about maintaining a successful blog is to provide regular, weekly content – at the least. If you are unable to provide regular entries, don't start blogging! Your blog will look outdated – and so will your business!*

## Twitter®/Facebook®/MySpace®/LinkedIn®/Flckr®

Some other social media venues include Twitter, www.twitter.com, Facebook, www.facebook.com, MySpace, www.myyspace.com, LinkedIn, www.linkedin.com, and Flickr, www.flickr.com/.

All of these reach out to customers with quick messages, photos, videos, sound bytes, and more. And each site has a specific purpose. But rather than go into detail about all of the different, social-media opportunities available, my advice is to explore what's available online. Conduct some research and see what sources will work for your PR goals.

And as you decide, keep in mind the time and effort that will be necessary for each, social-media-venue. Then, add the appropriate content, timelines and goals to your overall, PR Plan. This way, you won't waste time, and all of your social-media efforts will help you work towards your business success.

## Newsletters

It may seem like all businesses offer a newsletter, and there is a good reason for this. It's an easy, cost-effective way to communicate with your audiences and provide targeted messaging.

Best of all, a company newsletter allows you to easily build your own list of customers to sell to on a regular basis. Basically, you create your own database of people who "opt in" to receive your messages. Then, you build on these relationships and start to create a massive, marketing list of people specifically interested in your products and services.

Another benefit of a newsletter is that it enables you to communicate key messages, news and sales, and remind customers about your business *automatically*. While you focus on key priorities, you can set your newsletter to go out on a regular basis to provide valuable information to potential, new clients, media-members and others.

Newsletters provide an easy way to build customers and promote your business. To add one to your PR Plan, research various services available online such as iContact™, www.icontact.com, Constant Contact®, www.constantcontact.com, AWeber®, www.aweber.com, Emma®, www.myemma.com, Web Marketing Magic®, www.webmarketingmagic.com, and others to see what fits your specific needs and budget.

## Survey Reports/Study Results

If you can obtain interesting survey data or unique, study results, you will have valuable information to share with the media. Reporters are always looking for new statistics backed by a credible study or research group. And most people like to read results from the latest surveys.

Of course, you have an advantage if you are involved with a research or study group that generates in-depth data and reports on a regular basis. But if not, you can create your own data. To get started, focus on the needs of your customers and targeted reporters. Think of questions you can ask that will help you discover new information they will find interesting.

Then, create your survey with one of the easy and free or low-cost tools available online such as Survey Monkey®, www.surveymonkey.com/, FreeOnlineSurveys.com®, www.freeonline-surveys.com, KwikSurveys.com®, www.kwiksurveys.com/, and others.

Another option is to provide the survey questions in your regular newsletter with a deadline for responses.

With completed results, you have many opportunities. For example, you can:

- Offer your unique data as an "exclusive" to the media;

- Create a special, annual survey unique to your business and promote the results each year;

- Use the same, survey-results data twice by creating a year-end analysis of all of the surveys you conducted throughout the year; and

- Partner with pertinent organizations and businesses on a joint survey to create more buzz, and much more!

The possibilities are endless! Just be sure you can discuss the details of the survey process, how many people responded, who participated, etc. This will provide credibility for your final data. Otherwise, things can get ugly... fast.

If you don't have information to back up your survey, you may end up receiving negative publicity about your "faulty" results. Then, you'll be wasting time and effort managing a public-relations nightmare rather than a publicity coup!

## eReports/eArticles/eBooks

An eReport, eArticle or eBook simply refers to a document packed with valuable and interesting data for your target audience that you provide electronically.

These documents can be any length and are delivered via a Web site, e-mail, online newsletter, etc. You can also print the documents for tradeshows, events and regular postal-mailings.

To write an electronic document like this, simply collect current, survey-results, industry-studies, quotes, statistics, case-study information, and other, key data. Combine this information with your own expertise, insights and tips. Then, offer it to potential customers, media-members, investors, etc.

The main purpose of these documents is to entice potential customers to give you their contact information.

For example, by offering a free and "exclusive" eReport to people who register for your monthly newsletter, you can add to your database of opt-in, sales contacts and customers who want to know about your products and services.

And if you don't have time to write a report, you can always outsource this work to a freelancer. Just remember to provide original and current information that is user-friendly and per-tinent to the audience-members you are pursuing.

## Presentations/Speeches

If you spend the time and effort to prepare a presentation full of valuable tips and information, try to get as much out of it as possible. For example, write your presentation in a reader-friendly format, and create an electronic version.

Similar to the electronic documents mentioned above, you can post your presentation on your Web site and send it to perti-nent customers, potential advertisers or the press. This content will add value to your site, and give your target-market informa-tion they can't find anywhere else.

And if your presentation contains unique statistics, data or industry-trend information, consider pitching it to an appropriate media-member as an "exclusive." If you have not published the data yet, your presentation may be turned into a unique story that garners additional press and free advertising.

## Awards

One way to build credibility and awareness for your small business is to enter awards. And while some only take minutes to apply for, others can involve weeks of research, writing and editing.

Before pursing award-opportunities, decide which award-applications are worth your time and effort and if you have a chance at winning.

But note that if you win, or even become a finalist, you can promote this news to potential customers and mention the award in your marketing efforts. It gives you valuable, third-party credibility that you simply can't buy.

To participate in this publicity opportunity, look for awards specific to your industry. Then, review awards catering to small businesses as a whole. You'll also want to research unique awards related to customer service, marketing, human resources, technology, and other areas where your team excels.

Here are a few examples:

- The American Business Awards (The Stevie Awards)™

- The Ernst & Young Awards™

- Human Resource Executive of the Year™

- The Inc. 500™ via *Inc. Magazine*®

Now, if you are not a good writer and simply don't have time to enter an award, you may want to find a co-worker or hire a freelancer to help you with the application.

But note that you will probably still need to oversee the award-details. After all, many award-applications require sales statistics, customer testimonials, essays, photos, interviews with industry leaders, and much more.

After conducting your research, you may realize that there are many awards available for you to enter. To make it easier, add the entry-deadlines to your overall, PR Plan and calendar at the beginning of each year.

This way, you will be able to prepare your schedule accordingly for the application process. You'll avoid the stress of last-minute deadlines, and have more time to prepare a thorough entry that can significantly improve your chances of winning.

This may seem like a lot of work and just another item to add to your expanding "to do" list. With this in mind, you may want to wait to enter awards until your business grows and you have more resources for the application-process. But note that you may be missing out on some great award-opportunities now.

Not only is this potential publicity worth thousands in advertising dollars, but you also receive unique, third-party recognition and credibility to use in future, marketing efforts.

## Timelines

The last step in creating your action plan is to get organized and create a timeline that includes all of your PR activities for the year. By writing down your action steps with specific deadlines in advance, you will be more likely to save time and money, and reach your goals faster.

As you prepare your action-plan, it's important to remember the fast pace of the media-relations world. It can be very easy to move from one activity to the next and forget your original goals.

To stay on track, find a quiet space and review your overall, publicity goals and actions on a daily basis. Perhaps, you can start your day a little earlier or work later into the evening to make plans for the next day? Find what works best for you.

Ask yourself if you are progressing and spending your time adequately to reach your goals. If not, review your resources to figure out how you can make the changes necessary to succeed. Then, take action.

The key to saving time, money and working smart is to write down a plan-of-action with specific goals and timelines so you know what needs to be accomplished for success. And note that this will be an evolving document that changes as your business grows.

Think positively, review your list on a regular basis and get into the habit of working towards your goals each day. This process only takes a few minutes. But it can mean the difference between growing sales and staying at the status quo.

Once you have your plan ready, you can move forward quickly, and spend the appropriate amount of time on the right activities. This will not only help you focus, but you'll see more cost-effective results.

# CHAPTER 3

# WHO ARE YOU GOING TO CALL?

## WHAT MEDIA VENUES FIT YOUR GOALS?

At this point, you know what you want to accomplish, and have a PR Plan in place. Next, it's time to conduct media research. What media venues are going to help you reach your business goals?

If you haven't already done so, you can start by writing down your dream, media venues such as *"Oprah," "60 Minutes," "The New York Times," "The Wall Street Journal," "Entrepreneur,"* etc. After all, just because you are a new entrepreneur, there is no reason you shouldn't think big right away.

With this in mind, where would you really like to see a media quote about your business? Write down your top choices first. This will help you get into the right mindset, and start things in motion to actually take place!

Once you write down all of your top, media picks, it's time to find the other print, television, radio, and Internet venues that focus on the interests of your potential customers. In other words...

## WHAT DO YOUR TARGET AUDIENCE-MEMBERS READ, LISTEN TO AND WATCH REGULARLY?

To find out, there are several things you can do:

**1. Ask!**

The best way to get answers is to ask your current clients or potential customers directly for the information you need. You can make phone calls, run a simple survey, distribute comment cards, or send out questions via e-mail to an opt-in list.

**2. Search!**

By using one of the many, free online-search-tools, you can enter keywords and find popular media venues for your target audience.

For example, visits sites like Google, www.google.com, Yahoo!, www.yahoo.com, Bing!™, www.bing.com, and others related to your industry.

Enter keywords pertinent to your customers. For example, if you run a bakery, you may search for "cake baking media", "baking publications," "bakery magazines," etc. You'll probably be overwhelmed with the responses. But after some review, you'll be able to find the top media venues where your audience "hangs out."

**3. Get Help!**

If you simply don't have time to conduct this research, you can always outsource this work. And there are many options available depending on your budget.

There are college students who want part-time work, free-lancers who excel at research and outside marketing-firms that can get you exactly what you need.

However, it may be worth it for you to spend some time conducting research on your own. You'll get a better feel for your market. And this will help you create more interesting media-pitches, provide better products and services and form valuable relationships with your customers in the future.

But no matter how you develop your media list, it's up to you to study the various venues carefully. Ask:

- What are people talking about?

- What are the current industry trends and issues?

- What are the various tones and styles of the different media venues?

And since the business world is constantly changing, you'll need to review your list of venues on a regular basis, and edit it accordingly. This process is a lot of work, but it is a vital part of using your publicity activities to successfully reach your overall, business goals.


## WHO DO YOU CONTACT?

The next step in your research efforts is to study the people behind the venues on your media-list. You want to find the right person to contact at each venue to share your business story and begin a media-relationship.

To start, look for a Web site for the first media-venue on your list. Review the content and look for the people who talk about your industry, products or services. You'll probably find a specific writer, producer or editor who covers the stories and issues you want to share (their "beat") on a regular basis.

Once you find the right people, read, watch or listen to their current and archived stories. Study the style and tone of each press member and what she or he likes to talk about. By taking the extra time to learn these intricacies, you'll have a much better chance of creating a good story-pitch that the reporter, producer or editor will actually listen to and use.

## HOW DO YOU MAKE CONTACT?

As you go through your list of media venues, also look for the appropriate contact-information for the people you want to reach. Most Web sites list staff names and contact information. If not, simply call the main number and ask for the phone number and e-mail of the media-member you want to reach.

If this doesn't work, try conducting a more extensive, online search. You may find the information you're looking for via a YouTube® video, Twitter, FaceBook, Skype®, www.skype.com, or other Web site.

Another option is to purchase a media list via a service like Vocus®, www.vocus.com, Cision®, http://us.cision.com, Burrelles Luce®, www.burrellesluce.com, or one of the many other services available. However, these services may be expensive. If you have the budget and are short on time, these lists can be worth the expense. But I highly suggest you research the various services available before buying.

Check listings with The Better Business Bureau®, look for credible testimonials and compare benefits and pricing. And you'll want to go through this entire process again each year at renewal time. There are always new, updated services entering the market, and you may find a new service more specific to your budget and goals.

## CREATE A MEDIA DATABASE.

Once you have your list of media-venues and specific contacts at each, place all of this information in your own database. Use a software program like MS Excel®, Access®, Word®, or another program you feel comfortable using.

Your database should include simple tables that are easy to manage and update frequently. Also, it helps to have alphabetizing and spell-check functions and to be able to print user-friendly lists from your database.

Once you have your database, I suggest entering the following categories:

- Media Venue;

- Media Web Site;

- Contact Name;

- Contact Title;

- Contact E-Mail Address;

- Contact Phone;

- Contact Mailing Address;

- Notes; and

- Any Other Categories That Will Help You Stay Organized

While this takes a lot of time and effort, it is essential to create your own, personal list of media-contacts. This way, you can access information at any time, make updated notes about various conversations you have with the media and easily refer to your comments when necessary.

Your personal database will become your main source for media contacts in all of your future, publicity activities. After all, there can be a lot of turnover in the media industry so it is essential to stay aware of changes, update your notes accordingly and keep in touch with your media contacts. They may leave one venue to work at another, and you may have a whole new, publicity opportunity open up!

Also, note that this is your private list and should remain confidential. Although you could probably sell it for quite a bit of money, the media-contacts on the list will not appreciate it, and you could easily lose all of the relationships you worked so hard to create.

CHAPTER 4

# What Are You Going To Say?

## WHAT'S IN IT FOR THEM?

Now that you have a comprehensive, targeted media-list specific to your overall, publicity goals, it's time to develop specific pitches, or story ideas, for each media-member.

The days of sending out a blanket press release to a huge, contact-list are over. Your pitches need to be uniquely catered to each writer, editor, producer, or reporter.

With this in mind, open your media database and add a column for "Story Angles." Then, review your business plan and ask yourself some rudimentary questions:

- **What makes your business unique?**

Perhaps, you have a new product or service that is not currently on the market. Or, maybe you or your employees have a unique story to share regarding unique skills, background or working with the organization.

You may need to be creative and dig for this information, but it is well worth the effort. These are the "golden nuggets" specific to your business that media-members will be interested in hearing and talking about.

- **What benefits do you have to offer customers and the press?**

On the most basic level, media-members and potential customers are only going to care about what you have to say if there is something in it for them. Keep this in mind as you form all of your pitches. They want to hear about the benefits – not the features – that you have to offer.

Look at your products and services and really think about what you are providing others. And if you've already started offering your products and services, decide whether or not your customers are happy.

What do they like and dislike? Your answers will give you the underlying elements that will help develop word-of-mouth, fix issues before they expand into problems and grow your business.

- **Why will people be interested in your business?**

Once you know what your customers want and like about your products and services, it's important to focus on these qualities. These are the benefits they find interesting.

And if there are certain aspects of your business that you want to be "top-of-mind" to your customers when they think of your products and services, you will want to make these a priority in your publicity efforts as well.

Once you have these answers, you can create some great, story ideas. And as your business grows, it is essential to continuously focus on the needs of your customers at all times. Not only will this help increase sales, but it will also help you create targeted, publicity messages media-members will care about.

## HOW TO PITCH.

"Yikes!" Many of you may think that this is the scariest, unknown part of public relations. But don't worry. If you've done your homework, conducted the appropriate research, created a targeted, media list, and know the valuable benefits you offer your customers, it will be much easier.

### Preparation

To begin, review your list of benefits, unique qualities and the story ideas you created in your initial, PR Plan. Then, look at the first media-member on your list. How can you take the information you have and turn it into an interesting story idea specifically for him or her?

As you know, media-members are regularly bombarded with hundreds of e-mails, faxes and phone calls on a daily basis. This means that your story should be interesting and newsworthy – *to them and their audience.*

Think about current news, industry trends and unique activities occurring within your organization. And to get your creative juices flowing, ask yourself these questions:

- How does your business fit in with these current events and this particular, media venue?

- What information can you provide this media-member that is unique, interesting and pertinent to his or her beat?

- Do you have a customer who successfully used your services to increase sales and save time?

- Does that customer fit into a local region or niche covered by a particular, media-member on your list?

- Do you have any interesting events, tradeshows, speaking engagements, charity functions, etc. coming up that this particular media-member will be interested in covering?

Take some time to think through your story-ideas and how they pertain to each, specific media-member on your list. Then, write down your unique pitches for each media-member and when you plan to contact them. Add this information to your overall, PR Plan and schedule.

And while doing so, keep in mind that honesty is a must. While you can "spin" your business activities into interesting story-ideas, reporters will want you to back up your pitches with pertinent, customer testimonials, industry reports, news, research stats, or other credible data.

After all, your stories need to be truthful. Otherwise, you can get into a lot of trouble later... not only with the press and your customers, but with the law as well!

To give successful pitches, you really need to know what each of your targeted, media-members is looking for, how your business fits into current, industry trends and news, and why your story is unique.

And the only way to accomplish this is through research. But if you are short on time and need to contact a media-member right away, simply ask yourself the following question:

*"Why is this reporter going to care about this particular story and what I have to say?*

By looking for newsworthy stories and conducting the appropriate research, you will avoid wasting time, money and effort. Plus, you'll create valuable relationships with key media-members who can help publicize your business.

Unfortunately, there are no shortcuts in this pitching process. And you'll need to regularly review and create new, story angles as your PR Plan and business evolves.

However, these efforts are well worth it and can result in a feature story in a major publication or broadcast that will significantly boost sales and brand recognition.

## PRACTICE YOUR PITCH.

Now, if you don't like making sales calls or talking to people, pitching the media may seem like a very scary and daunting task. However, with some practice, your fears will subside, and you'll be able to share your story ideas effectively.

Before picking up the phone, here are three simple steps to help you prepare:

### 1. Review details.

Look at all of the information you've collected for each story-angle and media-member. Read the testimonials, statistics, trends, and other pertinent data relevant to your pitch. And while doing so, ask yourself why this reporter will find your pitch interesting.

Decide on the most important points that you want to convey, and right them down.

### 2. Speak out.

Now that you know what you want to say, practice your pitch aloud. Just like the elevator pitch you may have given when you first started your business, you want to be able to get your message out quickly, effectively and passionately.

In the privacy of a quiet room, practice what you will say to the reporter. If it helps, record your practice-session. Keep your pitch succinct, and figure out what sounds best.

Try not to memorize, but know the data so well that you can talk about it with enthusiasm and confidence. You want to sound like someone who is easy to-do-business-with and cares about the person's needs on the other end of the line.

### 3. Get feedback.

At this point, you may be ready to pick up the phone. But before you do, try your pitch out on a friend, co-worker or family member.

Ask if the pitch sounds interesting, when it may have become boring and what can be changed. Be prepared for criticism, and use this feedback to enhance your skills and presentation.

If necessary, return to step two above, and practice until you have a good pitch ready to go. Ugh! It's hard work, but soon you'll be able to talk to reporters with confidence and share valuable information.

And while it comes naturally to many, you may need a little more preparation-time. *But please don't get discouraged.* It can take a lot of practice and failed efforts before becoming a true, pitching pro.

However, it is a valuable skill to master. Not only can it help you increase media awareness and sales, but you can use these skills to win new customers, investors, sponsors, top job-candidates, and more!

# CHAPTER 5

# WHAT ARE YOU GOING TO PROVIDE?

To fully use the "power of PR" to meet your goals, you will need to prepare some written materials specifically for press members.

While you may have brochures, Web site pages, product samples, and other documents prepared for marketing purposes, you will also need to create an initial, media-kit and press-release.

Why?

Press members need different information about your business than potential customers – and they need it fast. By providing this data in a simple format that is easy to find, you will significantly increase your chances of garnering more media-attention and free publicity.

And it doesn't need to cost a lot of time or money. To start, keep it simple. You can always add complex videos, podcasts, white papers, postcards, and other, pertinent items later as your business (and budget) grows.

## WHAT IS A MEDIA KIT?

On the most basic level, a media kit is a collection of pages that provides reporters with the key information they need to know about your business quickly and easily. You will also see various types of media kits that address the needs of advertisers for magazines and other print materials.

But these are different than a "press" media-kit. For publicity purposes, we are referring to a media kit catering specifically to the needs of reporters, writers, editors, producers, and other media-members.

And you'll want to create an online version of your media kit so that media-members can access the information at any time with an Internet connection. This will make it easy for them to write their stories and meet tight deadlines. In addition, you won't need to spend the time or extra costs involved with printing and shipping fees.

However, for important events like live-conferences, speaking engagements, industry tradeshows and media-mailings, you will need to prepare a print-version of your media kit to handout and leave in the "press room" at the various events.

## WHAT SHOULD YOU PUT IN YOUR MEDIA KIT?

When members of the press look at your media kit, they should know the key benefits your business has to offer within a matter of seconds. Basically, you want to think about the main message you want to share and why your products and services are unique.

Your media kit should be simple, succinct and interesting. With this in mind, here are some key points you'll find in most media kits:

- **About Us or FAQ**

This section provides a brief synopsis about what your business or organization has to offer and why. This is where you provide company goals, mission statements, background data, and other key points that you want media-members to know about right away.

Here, you reach out to your target market and provide an interesting account of when and why the business was started, who was involved and any another other data about the history of your business.

You can write in brief paragraphs, bullet-points or in a letter-type format. Just remember to keep readers engaged with interesting stories and personal insights. Help them "see" the people behind your organization and feel like they are doing business with experienced professionals.

And if you are just starting out with your business, don't worry. You can write a few simple paragraphs, offer bullet-points or give the information in the form of "Frequently Asked Questions" (FAQ). If you have a lot of data to share, you can break it up into another section under a title such as, "Company History."

Use this section to provide the most unique and newsworthy elements about your business. This way, media-members will understand what you do, and why, quickly and easily.

- **Products and Services**

This is where you give information about all of the things you have to offer. But instead of talking about specific features, focus on all of the interesting and unique benefits that each of your products and services provide.

Make it easy for readers to see why they should use your products and services over those of the competition. In just a few seconds, they should know what you sell, how you can help them solve their problems and why they should buy from you.

- **Bios**

For this section, you'll want to provide information about each of the top leaders in your organization. Try to break down long biographies into short paragraphs, and highlight the key points you want media-members to know about the people behind your business.

Rather than just including the basic, boring data about birthplace, education, business experience, honors, and awards, give your biographies some pizzazz.

Add interesting stories from each leader, personal insights, quotes from clients about the person, hobbies, successful work-samples, and other, unique data. Not only will this information create a more interesting biography, but it will help make the leaders seem more approachable and real to potential customers.

Next to each biography, include a color photo of the leader. It should reflect the overall image the company is trying to project. This allows readers to see the faces behind the company. It also enables media-members to access photos online and use them in their stories at any time.

- **Company News**

As your business starts participating in more events, tradeshows, speaking engagements, and other activities, it's important to let press members and potential customers and investors know.

This is the section where you tell others about your company news. It includes your most recent press-releases (see detailed information on this topic later in this book), media-clippings (articles and stories where your business was quoted in print, online or on a television/radio broadcast), business successes or case-studies, upcoming events, and other, newsworthy activities.

And while you are putting your list together, there is one thing you need to keep in mind. While it's important to let others know about your media attention, be careful. A media-member may go elsewhere for a story if he or she thinks you have had too much media-coverage or if you recently did a story with a competitor!

However, if you make a conscious effort to think about the media clippings you include in your media kit (and who will be viewing it) prior to adding new information, you shouldn't have a problem with this issue.

- **More Information Unique to Your Business**

Once you have all of these basics ready for your media kit, think about other information you can add that is unique to your business.

Perhaps you want media-members to be able to access your company brochure, logos, promotional photos, ideas for future stories, newsletters, articles, and more? Add this information too. After all, you want your media kit to be a "snapshot" of your business that is easy to access and understand.

And if you don't have a lot of information to include, or aren't sure where to begin, check out media kits for other companies in your industry or businesses that you admire. You can see what you like most and clarify all of the things you need to include to make a good, first-impression.

After you complete your media kit, get feedback from others. Check for errors, and work with your tech team to post the media-kit online in the most user-friendly format possible. And be sure to add the appropriate contact information on every page so it's easy for reporters to get in touch with you.

Also, remember to add pertinent news and information to your media kit on a regular basis. After all, you want it to reflect the most current data about your business as possible.

For help finalizing your media kit, ask yourself these questions:

## Media-Kit Finalization Questions

1. What are the first things reporters see when they open the media-kit?

2. What is the overall message I want readers to take away from this particular page?

3. Is all the data current and correct?

4. Is the information easy to find, download and read?

5. Does the media kit reflect our organization's overall style and tone?

6. What will this particular media-member think when he or she sees this media clip?

7. After reading this, will reporters want to interview us?

8.  Is the media kit missing any key information that reporters will need to know?

9.  Is it easy to find business contact-information on the media kit?

10. How can I improve the media kit on a regular basis?

By reviewing your answers to these questions and making regular updates, you'll have a top-notch, media kit that will give press members valuable information and help you reach your PR goals.

## ONLINE NEWSROOM

### Create and Post a PDF.

Now that you have your media kit, create a final version in a portable document format, or PDF, for your Web site.

To do this, download a PDF program such as Software 955®, www.pdf995.com/, PrimoPDF®, www.primopdf.com, or another program. Simply follow the directions to turn a document or other file into a low-resolution PDF (for easy downloading). Then, save the document to your computer.

Once you create your media-kit PDF, add it to a section on your site specific to company news. Usually, this portion of a company's Web site is listed under "News," "Press Room," "Media," "News Room," "In The News," or other, similar name. Then, add a link to your News Room on every page of your Web site for easy access.

Basically, you want to make it as easy as possible for media-members to find this information at any time they visit your site. And your online newsroom is important.

After all, if you don't have an online newsroom, and your competition does, guess which company a reporter on deadline is going to write about first?

This is a valuable opportunity you don't want to miss. And to make it simple for you and get your information posted as soon as possible, here are the basic pages you'll want to include in your online newsroom to start:

| News |
| --- |

| Press Releases | Media Kit | Photos | In The News | Events |
| --- | --- | --- | --- | --- |

- **Press Releases**

On this page, list all of your press releases as soon as they are announced. Your most recent news should go at the top of the list noting the date and title of the release.

Provide the title of the press release and then create a link to a PDF-version of the release. This way, when someone clicks on the title of the release, the entire, PDF-version of the press release will open in a new window. The press release should be easy to access, download and print.

And it's important to update this page regularly with new press releases so your business appears to be current and news-worthy. If you have trouble adding a hyperlink, ask your Web designer or tech expert for help.

- **<u>Media Kit</u>**

When you first start your business, this Web page can simply consist of the words "Media Kit" with a link to the PDF version of your most current media-kit.

Later on, you can list all of the pages of your media kit separately with links to various portions of your site, contact information, media clips, and more.

But to get this posted as soon as possible, start out with a simple link. It is better to have the information posted rather than wait for a more complex, online media-kit with additional links, graphics and extra information.

- **<u>Photos</u>**

Once you have good, quality photos that you'd like to see in the press, you can share them with media-members on this portion of your site.

Print reporters will want high-resolution photos so you may want to make these available online. However, these photos take extra time to download and more server-space so you may want to offer low-resolution photos first, and provide high-resolution photos upon request.

Simply list the title of the photo, or post the photo with a link to the downloadable version. You can also say "Right click this photo to save and print." Again, ask for help from your tech team if you need it.

- **<u>In the News</u>**

In this section, you will want to list your press releases, major media-mentions, events, and awards.

- <u>Press Release Entries</u>

Start with your most recent press release. Provide the date and title with a link to the PDF of the press release as mentioned previously.

- <u>Major Media Mentions</u>

In a separate area, list all of your major media-mentions or "press clippings." Place the most current, or most important, clippings first. You'll either include links to PDF-versions of the clippings or links to the Web sites where the actual clippings reside.

But as you prepare these links, there are two things you need to be aware of before posting anything in this section:

## 1. **Do you have permission?**

Be sure that you have the appropriate approvals to post the media clipping on your site or link to it. You want to avoid copyright violations at all cost.

Simply send a request via e-mail to the appropriate producer or editor. Then, save the response in case you need proof of the approval in the future. Usually, it is not an issue if you link directly to the media venue's site and give credit to the venue. With this in mind, provide the media venue, title of the article and author's name whenever you post a clipping.

By following the appropriate procedures for clipping-approvals, you'll prevent future problems with media venues and possible, legal fees.

## 2. **What do reporters see?**

Your online newsroom is a great place to boast about your products, services and accomplishments. But always remember that it is for the media even though your customers, competitors, investors, etc. can access it. This means that competing media-venues may be visiting your site and reviewing the information.

With this in mind, there is the possibility that some media-members will not talk about your company after reading this page. Why?

As mentioned previously, some reporters may read the information and feel that your business has had too much media-exposure or realize that a media competitor recently wrote about your business.

To avoid this from happening, review your list of clippings online and in your print media-kit before it goes out. Try to get a feel for what reporters will think about the various sources listed. Ask yourself:

- Does it appear that you've had "enough" media coverage lately?

- Are you listing various, media sources rather than just competing newspapers or magazines?

This may be a "happiness problem" for you, but it is still something that needs your attention. Just remember that once you have numerous, media mentions, be smart about which clippings you "promote" online and list in your media kit.

After all, you don't want to defeat the purpose of getting more press from your online newsroom by being too proud!

- <u>Events and Awards</u>

For this Web page, you'll want to list all of your awards, presentations, tradeshows, and other events. To start, divide the page into the appropriate columns:

- <u>Awards</u>

Here, you will simply list any awards your organization has won along with the date and a link to the press release about the award.

If you've received press for winning several awards, be sure to add these mentions to your "Media Clippings" page too.

- <u>Events</u>

If your company participates in any tradeshows, speaking opportunities, presentations, Webinars, teleseminars, charity happenings, or other events, list all of them in this section.

Be sure to include future and past events with the appropriate date and a link to all of the pertinent details, photos, and contact information so that media-members can easily access this data at any time.

And note that it is important to regularly update this section. Although it takes extra effort, your "events" section reveals your business involvement in the community and awareness of current, industry trends. This page helps to promote the fact that your business is fresh and "newsworthy" at all times to the media.

Once you have all of these elements in your online newsroom, check to ensure that there is a simple link to your media-contact person on every page of your Web site. Again, you want to make it as easy as possible for media-members to know who to contact and be able to get in touch with you at all times.

It can be time consuming to keep your online newsroom updated. However, it is your major link to the press, and you want to make a good impression.

Plus, it is much less expensive to add current information online rather than to constantly create new, printed materials. And by adding new content on a regular basis, you'll obtain higher rankings with the search engines, and increase site visitors.

## PRESS RELEASES

We've already mentioned press releases a few times in this book. Now, it's time to give you the basic information you really need to create these newsworthy pages and enhance your overall, public-relations strategy.

### What is a Press Release?

When it comes to press releases, many new entrepreneurs don't know where to begin. Well, it doesn't need to be difficult.

Keep in mind that a press release is simply a written document announcing some kind of business news, announcement or event that you send to targeted media-members, partners, customers, investors, sponsors, and other pertinent people. It should be short, truthful, interesting, and easy-to-read.

Also note that most of your publicity is going to come from picking up the phone and pitching your story ideas directly to the media – *not from sending out press releases to the masses.*

And while you hope your press release will secure a front-page story and national media attention, that's just an added bonus that happens once in a while. Realistically, the whole point of producing a press release is to let your targeted audience know what is currently going on at your business and generate awareness.

More importantly, it is a great tool to remind media-members that you know the latest industry trends, provide beneficial products and services, are involved in the community, and can act as an expert resource at any time.

Plus, your press releases provide valuable "nuggets" of information about the growth and progress of your business, especially when you have a list of archived press-releases available via your online newsroom. This is important to potential investors, sponsors and advertisers who may want to work with you in the future.

## What Do I Write About?

If you have yet to send out a press release, your first one will most likely announce your business and the benefits you have to offer. You will provide your unique attributes and why you are starting your business. And you may want to offer a special, introductory offer or limited-time discount to increase interest.

Also note that you need to give yourself plenty of time to write and edit the release, decide how you are going to distribute it and pitch potential "exclusives" before sharing the information with the general media.

And after you send out your introductory release, you should plan to post at least one press release per month on an ongoing basis. I suggest this process in order to build awareness and relationships with media-members and your target market regularly. Plus, monthly releases can help your business look current and aware of the latest industry-trends.

But if you have trouble creating new ideas, refer to the previous section in this book on being "newsworthy." Think about current events, the message you want to convey, and most importantly, what you think media-members will really care about.

To get your creative juices flowing, here are:

## 25 Ideas for Media Pitches and Press Releases

1. What new products and services do you have that benefit others?

2. Do you have any customers willing to talk about their specific successes and experiences using your products and services?

3. What is going on in the world related to the benefits of your products and services?

4. Do you have a strong opinion about a recent news story?

5. What are the latest trends in your industry, and how does your business fit in with these changes?

6. Is your business involved in any upcoming events?

7. Are you and your employees involved in any charitable activities?

8. Can you create a new product, event or service with a partner, affiliate, advertiser, etc. and share joint publicity efforts?

9. Are you participating in a tradeshow?

10. Are you giving a presentation?

11. Can you create a unique contest that draws attention?

12. Do you have a free report or valuable content you can give away?

13. Are you having an online survey on an interesting topic?

14. Did you win an award?

15. Do any of your employees have interesting hobbies outside of work that you can relate to a newsworthy event or trend?

16. Did you recently hire a new employee to fulfill a special need or circumstance in your office?

17. Do you have an interesting, "Top 10" list to share?

18. Did you have a huge increase in sales, employees, customers, etc. in a short amount of time?

19. Can you promise fantastic, customer service, a solution to a problem, an outrageous guarantee, or another, interesting offer unique to your organization?

20. Did any funny or unique events happen within your organization that others will find enjoyable or interesting?

21. Do you have a prediction about a current event, news story or industry-trend that you can support with factual evidence?

22. Did you discover an unsafe business practice, scam or other issue that you need to share with consumers right away?

23. Are you providing a class, online seminar or teleseminar packed with valuable information?

24. Are there any holidays or special events coming up that you can use to create news (example: Administrative Assistant Day, Earth Day, Take Your Daughter to Work Day, Mother's Day, etc.)?

25. Did you just get some good press that you want to share with your target market that you can tie into an industry trend or current event?

Hopefully, this list will help jumpstart your brain with press-release ideas. Just remember that whatever you include in a press release needs to be of value to the press. If it focuses on you and your business alone, it is likely to go straight to the trash bin.

Now, let's write...

## HOW DO I WRITE A PRESS RELEASE?

First, take a breath. Writing a good press-release just takes practice and research. Like any new activity, you will get the hang of it over time.

Once you figure out the newsworthy information you want to share, it's just a matter of writing it down in the correct format and style.

And to make this process as simple as possible, I've broken it down into three, simple steps for you:

1. <u>**Review.**</u>

To get a good idea of how an effective press-release looks and sounds, review those written by competing companies and successful organizations. You'll find many examples on online newsrooms.

*Which press releases grab your attention and provide valuable information?*

By reading well-written releases, you'll learn what others "talk about" in their news, see the appropriate layout and be able to provide something different from your competition.

In addition to specific sites, take a look at the current press releases listed at newswire sites like PR Newswire®, www.prnewswire.com, The Associated Press®, www.ap.org, and BusinessWire®, www.businesswire.com.

A newswire service is simply a news organization that collects news and then sends it out "over the wire" to appropriate members, such as subscribing newspapers.

By looking at the press releases on these sites, you'll notice that they are written in a standard format. All you need to do is follow the same format.

For additional assistance writing a press release in the most accepted, "AP Style," check out the current issue of the *"Associated Press Style Guide,"* www.apstylebook.com. Full of correct grammar, punctuation, word spellings, and other, standardized styles, this user-friendly book will give you the information you need to write a professional, press release.

It will also help you standardize all other communications within your organization. For example, by having everyone in your organization follow the rules and usage definitions in the *AP Style Guide*, all of your copy will have the same style. And you'll avoid arguments about word-usage.

Best of all, the books is fairly inexpensive, and the latest edition is readily available at your local bookstore or online.

## 2. <u>Write a Headline and Sub-Headline.</u>

Now that you have a press-release format and style to follow, it's time to write a brief statement that communicates your main message. Write in the present tense, and avoid gimmicks and clichés.

Get to the point! Readers should understand what you are trying to say immediately and want to learn more.

Your headline should contain the key information about your release. Try to be specific and offer useful information that is unique. And when possible, include a sub-headline immediately after the headline.

This gives you an extra opportunity to provide additional and important information that you cannot fit into the headline.

Since most reporters will only read your headline, and possibly the sub-headline, spend most of your press-release writing time on these sections.

In addition, include your SEO keywords in your title so that the search engines can find your press release easily. I'll explain more about this in a few minutes. But for now, let's move on to the next part of your press release.

## 3. <u>Write a Few Paragraphs.</u>

At this point, you are ready to write the body of your release. But don't worry. Follow this simple process, and you will be finished before you know it!

- <u>Paragraph 1</u>

First, write down the location and date for your release:

City, State Abbreviation – Month, Day, Year –

Next, include short sentences that describe the "who, what, where, why, and how" of your news. If you want people to actually read your press release, be sure to include all of your key points in the first paragraph (with your Web site address, if possible).

Many Web sites will only reprint or show the first sentence of a press release with a link to the full release so it's very important to include the "why-will-anyone-care-about-this" information first.

And as you're writing, think about the key elements that your audience will find interesting. As mentioned previously, focus on benefits, not features.

Write content that your target audience will find interesting. Ask:

- How will people benefit from this news?

- What's in it for them?

- Why will they take the time to read this?

- <u>Paragraph 2</u>

Ok. Now, let's move to the next paragraph. Here, you can include a quote from the leader of your organization or from another expert pertinent to the release. And try to insert quotes that have value. In other words, avoid blatant statements like:

"We are excited about this partnership" or

"We are thrilled to be working with Business XYZ"

Of course you are excited about this news! You're sending out a press release about it, aren't you? Instead, provide valuable insights to the reader. After all, people usually add quotes to press releases to provide credibility and new information.

Offer statistics, personal tips and additional data that enhance your news whenever possible. This way, if your quotes are taken out of the press release and used in a story, they will offer a sampling of your news and provide credible data.

- Paragraph 3

In the next paragraph, describe your news in more detail and why it is important. You can also use bullet-points to explain the data in a reader-friendly format.

By including brief statements of data, it will be easier for media-members to get the information they need and quote your key points in their stories.

- Paragraph 4

Next, write additional data about the bullet-points you just listed, and include another quote if applicable. Then, end your release with the appropriate contact and follow-up information.

Now, take a look at your release. Is it a single page and easy to read? Are your main, news points easy to find and understand right away? If not, shorten your press release, and try to remove any extra "fluff" and unnecessary comments.

### 4. Add a Boiler Plate.

When you finish the main body of the release, include a brief section at the end, called the "boiler plate." This should be one, brief paragraph that provides important information about what your business sells, the Web site address and contact information. This way, media-members will know how to reach you and find more information about your business quickly and easily.

**Review your work.**

When you finish your release, take the time to check it for spelling and grammatical mistakes, factual errors, tone, and newsworthiness.

Have others proof it as well. Trust me. This is time well spent. Once the release is plastered all over the Internet, you cannot make necessary changes.

Obviously, this is just a simple outline to follow as a beginner. As you increase your press-release writing skills, you'll feel more comfortable adding and editing your releases and using the AP style.

And if you simply don't have the time to write a press release, it can be well worth it to hire an experienced, press-release writer. After all, you want your press release to project a professional image of your business and attract the right attention.

Plus, a writer who can incorporate the right SEO keywords into your release can significantly increase the number of media clippings, or "hits," your release receives, and track results.

But as a new entrepreneur, I know that you may not be able to afford this right now. No worries. It is possible to write your own press releases, even if you are not a good writer. However, be aware that it is going to take some research and extra effort on your part to produce a good result.

For help with your writing efforts, review successful press releases online and various grammar/writing books at your favorite library or bookstore.

## PRESS-RELEASE SAMPLES

As you prepare to write, note that some publicists use various, press-release-formats for different situations. For example, if you are simply announcing a new hire, internal promotion, upcoming event, or other item for a "newspaper calendar section" that is not necessarily newsworthy, you can simply share the information as succinctly as possible using the AP style.

Then, if you have news related to this announcement later, you can always issue another press-release.

For help in understanding the various formats, check out the templates on the next, few pages. The first, press-release template simply announces an event. And the next sample shows the actual press release for that event based on this template.

Following that, you will see some samples of standard releases. All you need to do is follow these templates, and you will be well on your way to completing your first press release! It's easy. Ready?

# EVENT-PRESS-RELEASE SAMPLE

Your Logo Here
FOR IMMEDIATE RELEASE

**Headline**
*Sub-headline*

What:     Name of the event and what it is about

Who:      Who is involved in the event? Give a brief description.

When:     Day of Week, Month, Date, Year

Where:    Address of Event Location

Why:      Brief description on why people should attend this event

Cost:     Include the price of tickets, parking information, refreshment costs, and other fees involved with the event.

Info:     Include a phone, e-mail and Web address where people can get additional information.

## About [Name of Your Company]

This is the boiler plate about your company and is included at the end of every press-release you create. You'll want to spend some time crafting a brief paragraph about your business. After reading this, people should know what your business sells, why you are unique, the benefits your products and/or services offer, and business contact-information. You can use the same boiler-plate information on all of your press releases.

# # #

(This mark shows that this is the end of the release.)

Media Contact: Your name, e-mail address, phone number

# **DANCE** GALLERY STUDIO

## FOR IMMEDIATE RELEASE

## Register Now for Summer Dance Classes for All Ages at Dance Gallery Studio, Ann Arbor

*Studio offers modern, ballet, jazz, hip-hop, and special workshops!*

What:     Dance Gallery Studio, Ann Arbor's only non-profit dance center, is now registering students for spring and summer classes May 22nd through August 19th.

Students ages 15 and up, novice through professional-level, can enjoy classes this summer from some of the region's top instructors in ballet, modern, jazz, hip-hop, and Pilates. Children ages 4 and up can enjoy ballet, modern and jazz and special dance workshops.

Why:     Learn a new skill! See why Dance Gallery Studio has served the community for over 20 years with the highest quality instruction and performances for all ages!

Where:     Dance Gallery Studio, 815 Wildt Street in Ann Arbor, MI www.dancegalleryfoundation.org

When:     Registration is going on now! Hurry! Classes fill-up quickly!

Cost:     Call the studio for prices. Register by May 8th and receive 10% off tuition. *Please see Web site for full details, www.dancegalleryfoundation.org*

Contact:     Kathryn Contessa, 734-747-8885 / dgkcontessa@sbcglobal.net www.dancegalleryfoundation.org

### About Dance Gallery Studio

Dance Gallery Foundation was established in 1984 and supports Dance Gallery Studio, the only non-profit dance center in Ann Arbor, Michigan. The studio offers students of all ages high-quality training in a non-competitive, nurturing environment with performance opportunities and an intensive, pre-professional training program. The mission of Dance Gallery is to produce, develop, and promote contemporary dance-performance, and provide dance training and educational experiences of the highest artistic quality. For more information on Dance Gallery Foundation, please see www.dancegalleryfoundation.org or call 734.747.8885.

# # #

Media Contact: Kathryn Contessa, dgkcontessa@sbcglobal.net, 734-747-8885

## STANDARD, PRESS-RELEASE SAMPLES

Your Logo Here
FOR IMMEDIATE RELEASE

### Headline
*Sub-headline*

City, State Initials – Date – Write short sentences including the newsworthy information about the release. Include all of the pertinent and unique data here (who, what, when, where, why, and how).

Next paragraph - Include a quote from the leader of your organization or from another expert pertinent to the release.

Next paragraph - Use this paragraph to describe your news in more detail and why it is important. Then, whenever possible, use bullet-points to explain the data and benefits offered.

- Possible bullet-point here written with an action verb
- Possible bullet-point here written with an action verb
- Possible bullet-point here written with an action verb
- Possible bullet-point here written with an action verb
- Possible bullet-point here written with an action verb

Next paragraph: Summarize and include another quote if applicable.

Next paragraph: Add appropriate contact and follow-up information here.

### About [Name Of Your Company]

This is the boiler plate about your company and is included at the end of every press-release you create. You'll want to spend some time crafting a brief paragraph about your business. After reading this, people should know what your business sells, why you are unique, the benefits your products and/or services offer, and business contact-information. You can use the same boiler-plate information on all of your press releases.

### # # #

(this centered mark shows that this is the end of the release)

Media Contact: Your name, e-mail address, phone number

# PRESS RELEASE SAMPLE
**(Note this press release was contained to one page)**

FOR IMMEDIATE RELEASE

**PrintingForLess.com Goes Green with 100% Wind Power**
*America's Print Shop Commits to Wind for All Its Energy Needs*

Livingston, MT – December 17, 2008 – PrintingForLess.com (PFL), www.printingforless.com, America's environmentally-friendly print shop, announced today that PFL now purchases 100% of its electricity from renewable, power sources. This means that every computer, printing press, folding machine, and light PFL uses is powered by a nearby wind farm. PFL is working with its local utility, Park Electric Cooperative, along with Basin Electric Power Cooperative's Prairie Winds-Energy in Motion Green Tag Program, to make this green initiative possible.

"Though wind-powered electricity costs a little more, we believe that as more businesses purchase energy from renewable sources, green power will gain momentum and go mainstream, eventually providing our country with the best of all worlds: energy that is clean, cost-effective and made in America," says Andrew Field, PFL President and CEO.

Why wind power? According to the National Renewable Energy Laboratory, http://www.nrel.gov/docs/fy05osti/37602.pdf:

• "Wind energy is economically competitive;

• Wind energy is a valuable crop of the future for farmers and ranchers;

• Unlike most other electricity generation sources, wind turbines don't consume water;

• Wind energy is an indigenous, homegrown energy source that contributes to national security;

- Wind energy is inexhaustible and infinitely renewable;
- Wind energy is clean energy that produces no emissions;
- Because wind energy's 'fuel' is free, it reduces the risk associated with volatile fossil fuel prices; and
- Wind energy has overwhelming public support."

"With our wind power, Forest Stewardship Council (FSC) certification for responsible forest management, and our other green activities, we are doing our part to help preserve the environment while providing high-quality marketing materials that our customers can be proud of," says Field. For more information on PFL's sustainable practices, visit http://www.printingforless.com/Green-Printing-Practices.html.

"We are pleased to welcome PrintingForLess.com to our Green Power Program," says Toni Cody, Park Electric Member Service/ Marketing Director. "By purchasing 100% renewable energy, PFL is helping to reduce greenhouse gas emissions and promote a cleaner and healthier local community." PFL is Park Electric's largest wind-powered customer.

To offer feedback, get more information on PFL's green initiatives, or boost your business with marketing materials that are easy on the environment, visit www.printingforless.com or call 800-930-6040.

## About PrintingForLess.com

PrintingForLess.com is the first commercial online printing company in the United States. Located in southwest Montana, PrintingForLess. com provides unmatched technical and customer support and instant online pricing and ordering for its full color printing services. Go to www.PrintingForLess.com for affordable, full-color printing services including: business cards, magnets, postcards, brochures, newsletters, posters, calendars, presentation folders, greeting cards, letterhead, and more. For additional information, please visit our Web site or call 800-930-6040.

### # #

Media Contact: Melanie Rembrandt, melanie@printingforless.com, (406) 823-7023

## A WORD ABOUT SEARCH ENGINES

As mentioned in the previous section, you'll want to use search-engine-optimization (SEO) keywords and phrases in your press release. This way, the search engines (like Google, Yahoo!, Bing!, etc.) will be able to find your press release online, and you'll get more attention for your news.

But don't worry. You don't need to be a technical guru to optimize your press release for the search engines. It's a very easy process that can bring big results. For your press release, just follow this simple process:

### Register for a Free, Keyword Search-Tool.

There are several sites available that offer free keyword searches at no cost. To start, check Keyword Discovery®, www.keyworddiscovery.com, Google, www.google.com, and Word Tracker®, www.wordtracker.com. Simply follow their online tutorials to learn how to search for keywords.

### 1.  Think like your target audience.

If you were a potential customer trying to find your products and services online, what words would you type into the search engines like Google?

Make a list of potential words. Then, enter these into your search-software and see what comes up.

### 2.  Place the words in your release.

Once you have a list of good SEO keywords, insert the key terms from your list into your press release. But avoid sounding too repetitive. You want your press release to make sense and provide valuable information without using the same keywords too many times.

### 3. Check your press release.

Not sure if you used your keywords too little or too much? After you've inserted the keywords, visit PR Newswire's free tool at www.icrossing.com/tools/calculator.htm.

You simply enter your keywords and your press release, and the tool will let you know if you have enough mentions of the keyword to be picked up by the search engines. Pretty cool!

That's it! You have a press release that is optimized for the search engines. Now, all you have to do is check your press release for readability, typos and grammatical errors, and you'll be good to go.

After your press release posts online, you can conduct a search for the keywords you placed in your release via Google or another search engine. See if your press release appears in the search results.

Depending on the outcome, you can keep the same keywords, or make changes and test different words for you next press release to see what works best.

### *What to Do With Your Press Release*

Now that you have your first press release ready to go, don't send it out immediately.

**Remember, press releases alone do not guarantee big, media placements.**

Press releases are a great tool for building buzz about your business. But before you spend too many resources on writing and distribution, review your goals, and research all of your

PR options (media-pitching, events, case studies, etc.). You may want to pursue other, publicity opportunities that will give you better results.

## HOW MUCH DOES A PRESS RELEASE COST?

New entrepreneurs often ask me how much a press release should cost to write and distribute. And the answer is that it can cost anywhere from nothing (if you take the time and effort to do it yourself) to thousands of dollars (depending on the services and distribution used).

*I think the real question to ask is... why are you sending out a press release in the first place?*

If you want to reach a specific audience, you may be better off talking directly to a reporter at a targeted media-venue without writing a release.

Once again, it all comes back to your specific goals and what you want to accomplish with your publicity efforts.

Now, if you want to announce some news to a large audience, remind media-members you have current products and services and get the word out quickly, a press release is probably the way to go.

And if you are not a skilled writer, I highly suggest that you find one to write your release for you.

After all, you want to make a good impression, and I'm sure you have core, business activities that need more of your attention and focus.

## HOW TO GET THE MOST COVERAGE POSSIBLE

Now, if you write your own press releases, try to get the most coverage possible from your hard work. To do this, follow these guidelines prior to sending out your release:

- **Review Your Media List.**

If you haven't already done so, figure out who you are going to approach about your news and ask:

*Who is going to be interested in an exclusive story that may ultimately help you reach your business goals?*

Create a list of these producers, editors, bloggers, reporters, and writers. Place the most important people at the top of your list. Dig around online, or call the media venues directly to discover the phone numbers, e-mails and other, contact-information for each media-member.

After developing your "exclusive-pitch" list, write down all of the additional media-members, partners, affiliates, employees, potential customers, etc. who will need to receive a copy of your press release.

This way, you'll know that all the pertinent people will get a copy of your latest news.

- **Develop Exclusive Pitches.**

Once you have your list ready, review previous stories written by the media-members at the top of your pitch-list.

What will they find interesting, and how can you pitch your story so that it is fresh and unique?

SIMPLE PUBLICITY

*And remember, each media-member will want different informa-tion so you will need to prepare a pitch specific to each person.*

**It's all about targeting the right person with the right pitch.**

To start, write down your key, talking-points for each me-dia-member. Then, practice what you are going to say during your phone-pitch so that you can get your message across suc-cinctly and with passion.

At this point, you will also want to create an e-mail mes-sage to follow up on your phone call. Simply write down all of relevant information in a short e-mail specific to each media-member. And at the bottom of your message, include your press release with a link to your Web site and more information.

And I highly suggest that you avoid adding attachments to your e-mails. After all, you don't know what kind of security-software the media-members use. Your attachment may get blocked and not even make it to the appropriate "Inbox"!

It's also helpful to send a test e-mail to yourself to see what your message will look like on the receiver's end. And write your e-mail message as a text message (choose "text" instead of "HTML" format in your e-mail system).

Graphics are nice, but you have no idea what kind of soft-ware program the recipient is using to read e-mail messages.

Keep it simple. This way, your e-mail will have a better chance of getting through to the media-member and provid-ing the information he or she needs quickly and easily.

- **Distribute the Press Release.**

How are you going to spread the word about your news? In addition to sending it to your personal list of contacts via e-mail, you will also want to look at various, distribution options.

To begin your research, review resources and information at sites such as PRWeb, www.prweb.com, PR Newswire, www. prnewswire.com, BusinessWire, www.businesswire.com, and The Public Relations Society of America (PRSA), www.prsa. org.

You'll also find many Web sites where you can post your release for free by doing a simple search. Look for pertinent media-venues online where your audiences hang out, and see if there is a section to post news-items.

Also, there are many niche sites and blogs that may cater to your target audience that have no-cost, news-posting areas.

To help you get started, check out the list of free, press-release-posting sites available on my Web site at www.rembrandtwrites.com. Note that these sites change frequently so you'll need to search for new, free sites and update your list on a regular basis.

## LOW COST, PRESS-RELEASE DISTRIBUTION

Next, take a look at low-cost, press-release-distribution options. With more media sites competing for your business, it is possible to distribute your press release on a national level for less than $100.00.

You can start with the lowest cost-options on these distribution sites and then pay for extra services (such as podcasts, photos, videos, etc.) as needed.

If you are announcing an event, promotion, or other activity that you don't think has significant, news potential as a unique and fresh story for reporters, you may want to use this option.

Your press release will be distributed, and you'll remind your key, audience members and the media that you have fresh news. Plus, your press release will be "picked up" by the search engines giving you additional, online exposure.

For more information on low-cost-distribution services, checkout PR Web at www.prweb.com and conduct an online search for a service that fits your specific needs.

In addition, you may want to talk to a representative about your distribution and editing options at PR Newswire, www.prnewswire.com, and BusinessWire, www.businesswire.com.

Many times, these services provide smaller distribution-options at lower costs. And since it can be difficult to figure out fees for a specific, distribution list for your release, the customer service representatives at these services can guide you in the right direction, edit your release and help you save money.

In addition, many of these services offer discounts to members of various groups and organizations. Look for "PR Package Specials" on the Web.

You may be able to waive registration fees, or take advantage of a specific coupon or offer too. The time you take to research various options can be well worth it.

## FULL COVERAGE, HIGH COST PRESS-RELEASE DISTRIBUTION

If you are announcing your new business for the first time or have some particularly, newsworthy information to share, you may want to consider spending more money on a national release via a wire service.

Journalists and media-members regularly review press releases distributed by the wire services (The Associated Press, PR Newswire, BusinessWire, etc.). And all of the public companies use these services in order to provide key information to their investors.

With these services, you pay according to the length of your release and the distribution-level you choose. To give you a rough estimate, you may pay a membership fee of about $195.00. Then, you pay an initial cost for national distribution for the first 400 words plus $185.00 or more for each additional 100 words in your release.

You can also purchase various upgrades including photos, editing, videos, audio, podcasts, online media-rooms, and more.

These services can take a significant chunk out of your budget. But it may be worth it. Your release will receive more credibility and coverage by using an official, wire service. Plus, you can receive guidance from expert editors and staffers who work with press releases on a daily basis.

But if you decide to go with a big, national distribution, confirm that your press release is written well and conveys some unique, newsworthy information that press members will find interesting. Otherwise, you won't receive much media-coverage and will end up wasting your money!

## CHAPTER 6

# Маке Соптаст!

## THE SIMPLE SECRET TO GETTING PRESS

As you can see, public relations can take a lot of effort. But if you just don't have time to go through all of the steps mentioned in previous chapters, there is one thing you can do to help generate media coverage right away...

***Pick up the phone!***

That's right. You will get the most media coverage by simply picking up the phone and sharing your story with the right media-member at the right time.

*The secret to garnering huge, media attention comes down to having a simple, telephone conversation.*

Not only will your call help you create a relationship with a press member, but via phone, you can accurately convey your passion, excitement and expertise about a newsworthy idea.

And if you already feel comfortable doing a phone pitch, and know the media-member you want to pursue, you can go ahead and start calling. But be sure you know what you are going to say in advance. Otherwise, your "fast approach" can backfire, and the reporter may not want to speak to you for several months – or ever again!

Now, phone pitching may sound horrifying to many of you. But don't worry. With a little practice, you can become a pro and wonder why you were so nervous about it in the first place!

## GET READY TO PITCH!

To help you get ready for your first media-call, let me walk you through three, simple steps:

### 1. Review.

You've already conducted tons of research and know which media-members you want to pursue. All you have to do is review your research and the newsworthy information you want to share.

Check current trends, articles written by the pertinent media-members on your list and how your idea fits into their beats. It is also wise to prepare two or three, different story-ideas in case the reporter is not interested in your first choice.

### 2. Practice.

Ok. Step one was pretty easy. Now, all you need to do is figure out your key talking-points. Remember, the reporter needs to know why your idea is unique and offers value to his or her audience.

With this in mind, figure out how you can get your message across quickly and with passion and enthusiasm. Write down short bullet-points that cover the important information.

You can use this as a guideline to create your talking points:

## Talking-Points Guideline

- **What is the main point I want to get across to the reporter?**

  Your sample thoughts: I am introducing myself as a new entrepreneur and expert-resource in the area of widgets. In fact, I have a great story about how I created my business after working with my seven-year-old son on a science project.

- **How am I going to convey my idea?**

  Your sample thoughts: I don't want to take up your time, but I thought you should know about this new widget because it reduces all household pollutants by 98% in only three hours.

- **Why will the reporter care about what I have to say?**

  Your sample thoughts: My widgets provide a brand new, unique way for people to reduce their carbon emissions. One of my clients saved $10,000 using it. And I know you recently wrote about recycling so I'd like to give you the exclusive story.

Do you see how each talking-point provides valuable information that peaks the reporter's interest? Really think about these issues as you create your pitch because you only have one shot to make a good, first-impression.

Once you have your talking-points ready, practice what you are going to say out loud. Pick up the phone, and pretend you are talking to the reporter. Give your pitch, and think about the various responses you may receive.

## Sample Introduction-Script

Here's a sample introduction script to help you get started:

You:        "Hi Bob. My name is John Doe, and I just started a new widget company here in town. We provide various types of widgets made with a unique wood from Michigan and have over 50 years of experience in this industry. Would you like to receive our latest news and information?"

Reporter:   "Sure."

You:        "Should I send it to you via e-mail, or give you a call when news comes up?"

Reporter:   "E-mail is best."

You:        "What is your e-mail address?

Reporter:   It's _____.

You:        Thank you so much for your time Bob. I look forward to sending you some valuable news and information in the future for your readers. Please consider me as an expert-resource for future articles as well."

To prepare further, practice with a friend, family member or co-worker. Do some role-playing, and have your buddy act as a nice reporter, a difficult editor or a time-constrained producer. You may want to record your practice interviews to see how you look and sound in the process, and jot down where you need improvements.

Another important note is to try to get the reporter's e-mail address and direct phone number while you are talking to him or her, if you don't already have it. This will make future communications much easier.

Now, all of this can be time-consuming and a lot of work. But it is well worth the effort. After all, it can mean the difference between sounding professional and getting a story or clamming up and missing out on a great, media opportunity!

### 3.   Pick Up The Phone!

Great! You should be ready to make the call. Right before dialing, review your notes, and check to see what time-zone you are calling. After all, you want to call when the media-member will be in the office. And if you are trying to reach a producer for a live, morning broadcast, obviously you do not want to call while the program is actually on the air.

If you are new at this, I highly suggest that you start with a local media-member who is part of a smaller venue. This way, if you really mess up, it won't be on a national level.

Also, if you get an answering machine, simply leave a brief message with your name, business name and phone number. You will also want to state why you are calling in just a few sentences.

For example, you might say something like this:

"Hi Michael. My name is John Doe, and I am a new entrepreneur with <u>Name of Company</u>. I would like to offer you an exclusive story and act as a resource for your future columns.

You can reach me at 000-000-0000, and my e-mail is _____. Thanks for your time, and I hope to hear from you soon."

Now, take a deep breath and dial the number for the media-member on your list. Good luck!

## AFTER THE PITCH

Phew! That's over with. How did your call go? If you:

### A. <u>Couldn't get through and left a message.</u>

Immediately record this information in your media database.

- Who did you leave a message with?

- When did you call, and what did you say?

Make a note to contact this reporter again in one to five business days. Then, send an appropriate follow-up e-mail like this one:

## Sample, Follow-Up E-Mail

**Subject Line:** Per phone message regarding widgets in your column (Note: Mention that you left a message and add some succinct, newsworthy tidbit in your subject line.)

Hi John,

Per my phone message, I have an original, fresh story to offer you regarding a lady who was once homeless. She used my new widget and is now living a wealthy, happy and healthy life in the Bahamas.

She only spent $5.00, and the widget changed her life within 15 months!

This story has not been covered by the media yet, and I would like to discuss it with you further.

Please visit Web site address link for more information and feel free to contact me at your convenience.

Thanks very much,

John Doe
President
Company Name
E-mail address
Phone Number
Address
City, State  Zip Code

## B. <u>The reporter asked you to call back in a week</u>.

If a reporter asks you to get in touch at a later date, this is a *good* thing. He or she may be interested but just not have time right now to focus on your story-idea.

If this is the case, be sure to note this information in your calendar and media database. Then, CALL BACK AT THE APPROPRIATE TIME!

If you forget to call back, you will miss out on a golden opportunity – not only for a potential press-mention, but to begin a new and valuable media-relationship.

## C. <u>The reporter asked for more information.</u>

Woo Hoo! This is definitely a good thing and the response you hope for when pitching.

As soon as you hang up the phone, gather the appropriate information the reporter asked for and send it to him or her immediately – in the format requested. *Speed is of the essence.*

And after you send the information, follow up the next day to see if the reporter needs anything else. If you leave a message and don't hear back from the reporter, make a note to contact him or her on a regular basis (about once a week) without being annoying.

Media-members are busy so you need to gently remind them that they asked you to contact them about a great, story idea that you sent them.

And each time you talk to the reporters, have fresh stats, news or information to share. Let them know that you can be a valuable resource.

Also, treat them like you would like to be treated. Don't be phony, annoying or pushy. Just act natural, and treat this introduction like a new, business relationship. This way, you'll have a win-win situation.

## D. **The reporter wasn't interested.**

If the media-member you called was not interested in your story idea, don't worry. At least he or she now knows who you are.

Make a note about your conversation in your media database. Did you ask if it would be o.k. to contact them with other, pertinent story-ideas?

If so, you'll want to contact them on a regular basis with a new and pertinent story-idea just for them. Place this information in your calendar so you don't forget. Then, move on to the next media-member on your pitch list.

As you can see, you may have a lot of luck with your first call. You can place a story right away or not hear from a media-member for several months. Usually, it is a long process, and you need to be patient and persistent.

The point is that you need to start getting your name out there, and let your target media-members know that you are a great resource and have valuable information to share – at any time.

Once you start this process, you will be well on your way to publicity success.

## PERFECT YOUR PITCH.

As you hone your pitching skills, there are a few things to keep in mind. Pitching the media is an art, and it takes time to perfect your tone and style.

*But it doesn't need to be difficult.*

Before creating a pitch, always ask yourself:

**Why is this media-member going to be interested in what I have to say?**

Just by reviewing your response to this question before moving forward on a pitch, you can save yourself a lot of wasted time and effort. Plus, it will help you make a good, first-impression.

And after you've talked to the media and have some practice pitching, ask yourself the following questions:

- What do media-members really think of you?

- Do they like working with you?

If your answers are negative, you probably need to make some changes. Are you being annoying or contacting the wrong reporters with generic information they couldn't care less about?

Even if you have a good rapport with reporters, regularly ask yourself these questions to stay on track. You always want to provide newsworthy information and think...

*"What's in it for them?"*

With this in mind, check out this list of...

## THINGS YOU SHOULD NEVER DO WHEN TALKING TO THE MEDIA:

- Tell lies;

- Send a generic, press release to hundreds of media venues at once;

- Provide boring, story ideas that focus on features rather than benefits;

- Offer pitches that have nothing to do with the reporter's beat;

- Give an "exclusive" story to more than one reporter (they'll find out!);

- Inform reporters that you'll send information you never intend to deliver;

- Ignore their calls or urgent e-mails;

- Cancel interviews at the last minute;

- Rewrite their article for them;

- Offer to provide one resource/expert/spokesperson and then offer another without letting them know;

- Provide confidential information that is "off the record" (it won't be); and

- Make constant, follow-up-calls.

With this list in mind, also note the following:

## THREE KEY ISSUES THAT CAN RUIN A BIG PUBLICITY WIN:

### 1. Never say "No Comment."

While this may be the easy response to an uncomfortable interview-question, try to avoid saying it. These two simple words can have negative connotations and minimize your credibility.

Instead, try to maintain control of the situation as much as possible, and respond in a positive, upfront manner.

For example, be honest and explain why you cannot give an answer. You might say something like, "I can't answer that question because it is not our policy to divulge private, client information."

This way, you'll reaffirm your authority without divulging information. Stressful media-requests can pop up when you least expect it so it is a good idea to review how you (and your team members) will deal with various situations in advance.

### 2. Avoid opinionated responses without fact.

Think of your responses in terms of sound bites or the quotes that media-members will pull out of your interview.

You want your statements to be truthful and build positive awareness for your small business. Remember, reporters may only use portions of your quotes in a story.

Therefore, you want to be sure to speak in complete sentences and project clear messages every time you open your mouth.

If you do not know an answer to a question, try not to guess or rattle on with a long, opinionated answer. Instead, simply say something like, "I don't have that data now, but if you'll give me your e-mail address, I will get that information to you as soon as possible." Then, when the interview ends, be sure to follow up with that reporter as soon as possible.

### 3. Avoid saying "off the record."

Keep in mind that anything you say to a reporter can appear in the press. Even if you have a solid relationship with a media-member you trust, it is always a good idea to be aware of what you say at all times.

In fact, it's smart to avoid stating anything you don't want publicized. There is always the temptation to print the latest "gossip" and "insider, news tip."

With this in mind, I always advise clients to stick to their publicity training and key messages when speaking to media-members – at all times and places.

After conducting extensive research and preparing your story-ideas, you will be ready to contact the media.

You can write a press release announcing your new business, and simply call or e-mail the appropriate media-member with a simple introduction.

But before you contact the media, there are a few questions you should avoid asking in order to be professional and build positive relationships:

## TEN SIMPLE QUESTIONS YOU SHOULD NEVER ASK A REPORTER:

1. My client just created a new product, will you write about it next week?

2. What are your columns about?

3. How do you spell your name?

4. Will you write a feature story about our small business?

5. We are having a press event tonight, can you come?

6. Did you get my fax?

7. Are you going to write about the press release I just sent to you?

8. Our CEO is available to speak to you now. Do you have 30 minutes to hear his story?

9. Can I proof your story before it goes to print for errors?

10. The local paper and *CNN* just did a major story about my client. Would you like to do the same story too?

These are just a few of the numerous, annoying and frivolous questions reporters receive every day.

What others do you have to add to this list?

## PITCHING-TIPS

Ok. We've covered many of the key items you should avoid if possible when communicating with media-members. In contrast, here are some key points to keep in mind to sound professional, provide valuable information and help secure more press-coverage:

- Give reporters valuable, honest stories that are current and unique to their specific audience;

- Conduct the appropriate research, and learn the media venues and reporters' beats;

- Know your business well, and offer current data on industry trends and news;

- Offer valuable, company information at all times via an online newsroom;

- Provide requested photos and other data quickly;

- Keep scheduled appointments, and provide as much information as possible;

- Be available when needed; and

- Maintain a professional relationship where you respect the reporters' time and deadlines.

Discover as much information as possible before you pick up the phone. And if you are just starting out with your PR efforts, you may want to keep this list on top of your desk for easy access.

This way, you'll remember what you need to do, and improve your chances of getting some good publicity. But more importantly, media-members will start to realize that you are a valuable resource for future stories.

And that brings us to our next section...

What do you do when your hard work pays off, and reporters start calling for interviews (other than do a happy dance!)?

## HOW TO DO INTERVIEWS

Congratulations! A reporter just called you and wants to interview you for an upcoming article. This is fantastic news! But try not to get too excited. Remain calm and ask yourself:

*Am I ready to talk to this reporter <u>right now</u> about this subject?*

## BEFORE THE INTERVIEW

More than likely, you will need a few minutes to get your thoughts together, review your notes and figure out what you want to say.

Whenever possible, ask the reporter if he or she has an immediate deadline. If so, ask if you can finish what you are doing very quickly and promise to call the reporter back within ten minutes.

Then, take a deep breath.

Think about the key messages you want to convey about your company. Look at the talking-points "cheat-sheet" you created earlier, and consider the following:

1. What is the goal of this interview?

2. What do you want people to take away from this story when they see it?

3. Never say anything you don't want to see in print ("off the record" often means nothing to a reporter!)

4. Never say "no comment." Instead, be prepared with an answer or use a bridge (more on page 109).

5. Check with your attorney and other team members on the current statistics and information you are allowed to share with the press.

Basically, you want to take a moment to prepare whenever possible. This will help you say the right things, cover all of your important points and give a better interview.

And if you already work with someone who handles your media-relations, contact that person immediately. He or she may have some important points and last-minute reminders for you that you need to stress during the interview.

*When you are ready, be sure to call the media-member back as you promised. If you don't act quickly, you can lose out on the opportunity or ruin a valuable, media relationship for future stories.*

## DURING THE INTERVIEW

As you speak to the reporter, look at your notes, and think about your responses. You'll want to mention your Web site address, book title, e-mail address, or other, important contact-information so that people who see the story know where to contact you.

In addition, here are some additional, key points to remember for your interview:

1. **Be Honest.**

    If you don't have an answer for a question, simply say something like this:

    "I don't have that information right now, but I can get it for you as soon as possible."

    (After the interview, be sure to provide the information requested as soon as possible.)

2. **Listen Carefully.**

    While having an interview, it can be easy to be distracted due to excitement and nerves. To avoid this, try to keep your notes close by. Listen carefully to what the reporter is asking. And take a breath before giving your response.

    Then, try to answer his or her questions correctly while steering the conversation in the direction you would like it to go.

3. **Stay Positive.**

    Avoid negative remarks if possible. If you stay positive, you will have a much better chance of controlling the interview and communicating your ideas and viewpoints. (Note that many business owners use negative remarks to project a certain image and build buzz. But these kinds of comments should be part of your overall, PR Plan and discussed prior to an interview.)

    Also, know that it can be difficult to hear, understand or talk to many reporters due to bad connections, speaking patterns, thick accents, and many other factors.

When this happens, do your best to be considerate, patient and professional. Try to conduct the interviews on a good, land-line phone connection in a quiet place so you can focus on the reporter's needs. If you can't hear a reporter, let him or her know immediately.

**4. Correct Incorrect Information.**

If a reporter states information that is incorrect, be sure to correct him or her with the right information immediately.

Back up your statements with facts, statistics, reports, etc. You want to make sure the reporter has accurate data so you can help avoid being misquoted.

**5. Stay in Control.**

No matter how controversial the conversation becomes, or how much the reporter tries to "dig" valuable secrets and negative responses out of you, keep your head at all times.

It is important to answer questions truthfully. But at the same time, you want to try to manage the conversation and discuss your key, talking points.

To do this, you may want to create bridges and use flags:

## Create Bridges.

To become an excellent interviewee, you may want to study bridges. These are words you use to transition from one point in a conversation to another.

You can use bridges to easily move from one sentence to the next, and help guide a discussion in the direction you want it to go.

To use a bridge, first, respond to the question. Then, use the appropriate phrase to segue into the point or topic you want to make.

Here are a few examples:

- "That's a good point, but I'd like to say..."

- "In addition, our research shows that... not only have we grown sales, but we have also..."

- "I appreciate your opinion, but we feel that the important issue is..."

- "That's an interesting point, but the key issue is..."

- "You say that, but it's not quite right..."

- "We don't think that's the case, we believe that..."

Obviously, you want to practice using these transitions so they sound natural and work smoothly. By knowing your key marketing-messages and creating bridges, it will be much easier to provide intelligent responses while guiding the conversation.

## Use Flags.

In addition to guiding the interview with bridges, you can also use "flags" to stress the importance of a point you are making. As in waving a flag for attention, flags are simply phrases that add emphasis to what you are saying.

Some examples include:

- That's an important point, but I think the key issue to focus on is...

- That is a relevant factor, but the most important thing for people to remember is...

- The critical factor here is...

- The most important issue to focus on regarding this event/debate/action is...

You get the idea. If you have an important opinion, issue or fact that you really want the media-member to include in the interview, be sure to emphasize it in very simple terms.

But remember, you want to sound natural at all times. Try to include a flag as subtly as possible. Once again, you'll want to practice this tactic prior to an interview in order to sound professional while getting your point across.

Even though the final, media quote is out of your control. You can manage your sound bytes (your edited quotes that appear in the final, broadcast story) and guide the interview in the direction you want it to go.

Take your time to give well-thought-out responses that are positive in nature. If not, you may be misquoted, and your responses may be taken out of context. Then, you'll end up handling calls for a negative, media crisis rather than calls for new business and additional interviews!

For example, reporters may ask you questions about a current crisis or problem at your company. When this happens, tell them the truth about the issue. Then, focus on the positive activities your team members are taking to remedy the problem so that it doesn't happen again.

After that, you can start discussing other, positive benefits about your organization, upcoming activities and new products and services that help others in some way.

### 6.  Talk in Sound Bites.

As mentioned previously, media-members will often edit your quotes and only use the comments that fit in with their stories. You usually have no control how your quotes will be cut and used in the story so try to give complete sentences for each response.

This way, it will be more difficult to edit the quotes without including all of your key points in the sentence. And you'll have a better chance of being quoted correctly in the press.

### 7.  Take Notes.

While you are on the phone with the reporter, try to take notes on what you discuss. This will this help you remember your conversation the next time you speak to this reporter.

More importantly, it will help you do the appropriate follow-up, provide any additional information requested and input specific notes about the reporter (and your conversation) into your personal media-database for future reference.

### 8.  End the Interview the Right Way.

When the interview is coming to a close, tell the reporter that you are available for additional questions via phone or e-mail. Ask if he or she needs photos, and offer yourself as a future resource pertaining to your area of expertise.

*Give the reporter your personal, contact information, and be sure to get his or her phone number and e-mail address if possible.*

Also, ask when he or she thinks the story will be published or go live. You'll want to make a note of this so you know when to look for the story and possibly order copies.

Finally, thank the reporter verbally.

## AFTER THE INTERVIEW

### Send a Thank-You Note Right Away.

Immediately after you hang up the phone, or as soon as possible, send a quick, "thank you" via e-mail to the reporter.

In your note, provide your contact information, any requested information, photos, reports, etc. Also reiterate the fact that the reporter can contact you at any time if he or she needs a resource or information for a future story.

If the reporter didn't request additional information, tell him or her you'd be happy to send photos, reports, other contacts, etc. if necessary.

*And don't send attachments in your e-mail unless the media-member requested you to do so.*

You don't want to slow down the reporter's e-mail system or provide an overload of unnecessary information.

Now, if you have a publicist working for you, contact him or her first when you are finished with your interview. Share exactly what you discussed, how it went and when you think the story will go live.

Then, if you have a good publicist, he or she will conduct the follow-up directly with the reporter for you, send the appropriate information, provide any corrections (in case you gave some faulty information), and send the right photos.

He or she will also track the progress of the story, report pending, publish or air dates and help obtain copies for you.

When you are finished with your interview, take a moment to review how you did and what you can do to improve next time. By taking notes each time and practicing your skills regularly, you can reduce your nerves and actually look forward to your next interview!

## SPECIAL NOTES ABOUT TELEVISION AND RADIO INTERVIEWS

When you have a phone interview with a reporter, it is easy to look at your written "talking points" and take notes during the interview. But for television and video interviews, you may not be able to have your "cheat sheet" in front of you for help.

If you are just starting out, it's best to conduct a few phone interviews first. Then, you can move forward to live or recorded appearances which offer their own unique challenges.

To prepare for these types of interviews, here are a few key points to keep in mind:

**Practice.**

To conduct a good interview, you want to practice giving your key message while using both bridges and flags – without referring to your notes. You want to feel confident about what you are going to talk about and be able to speak clearly and concisely without sounding rehearsed.

For some, this comes very easy. But for most of us, it takes some time and effort to become a good interviewee. Start by practicing with a friend, family member or co-worker.

Then, conduct some interviews with a small, local press-member if possible. It is important to have some actual, interview practice and be prepared prior to reaching out to large, media venues.

After all, you don't want to make a bad impression and have to deal with cleaning up the aftermath of the wrong quote or company statistic being released. Instead, you want to feel confident and use the power of the press to your advantage.

In addition to all of the interview-preparation discussed previously, it's essential to focus on how you will look and sound for recorded interviews. This may seem simple, but if you have never been in front of a camera or talked into a microphone before, you have some work ahead of you.

## Create a Video.

To start, schedule some time to practice your interview skills in front of a video camera. Have a friend, co-worker or family member ask you various questions while recording your interview.

Then, review the results and ask yourself a few questions.

## Interview Review

- How did you look? Do you project the professional image you want others to see?

- How did you sound? Can people understand what you are saying?

- Did you have any strange habits you were unaware of until now? Do you bite your lip, repeatedly say, "Um," move your hands too much, stutter, etc.?

- Did you speak in complete sentences and "sound bites" for editing purposes?

- Did you convey your main message?

- Which questions did you have difficulty responding to and why?

- What changes can you make to improve your interview?

Once you review your performance and make changes, conduct another taped interview, and repeat the entire process.

Then, have outside associates, a hired media-trainer or appropriate co-workers give their insights, tips and reactions. You may even want to offer confidential, survey forms to obtain truthful, anonymous responses, comments, and suggestions about your performance.

This is a lot of work. But each time you practice, you will fix bad habits, improve your skills and feel more confident. And it will be well worth your time and effort.

After all, would you rather make mistakes on national television or in the privacy of your own office where you can easily press the delete button?

## What to Wear

As part of the interview process, you'll want to prepare something to wear in advance and have it ready to go. This is one thing you can control that will give you more confidence.

And it's fairly simple. Just think about the image you want to project, and dress accordingly.

Here are some Do's and Don'ts to help you prepare your outfit:

### Don't Wear:

- Shiny ties or blouses.

    You want to make it easy for the lighting director to focus on you without a distracting glare. Plus, shiny items tend to look like they are made of a low-quality material on screen.

- Bold patterns.

    Try to avoid any shirts, ties or blouses that are "busy" and distracting with lots of stripes, prints, colors, etc. You want people to listen to you instead of looking at your shirt or tie.

- Lots of jewelry.

    When it comes to television, try to keep your earrings, bracelets, watches, rings, etc. to a minimum (unless you are trying to portray a certain image, selling the jewelry, trying to draw attention to the jewelry, etc.). Not only can the shine be distracting and noisy, but it can get in your way and cause lighting issues.

- All white or all black.

    You don't want to fade into the background, look pale or cause additional, lighting issues. On this note, you may want to ask the producer if there are any colors you should avoid wearing.

- Clothing with messages or advertisements.

    While you may love your favorite concert t-shirt or hat that advertises a product or service, a political-view or your favorite charity, this is not the right thing to wear for a television-interview.

    Not only is this unprofessional and distracting, but the producers will probably need to block out the name on your shirt to avoid copyright/trademark violations or negative, viewer comments.

- All of your logo apparel.

    While it's o.k. to wear a hat or shirt with your business logo on it for some television appearances (coverage of an outdoor charity-event, casual interview, tradeshow, etc.) try to avoid it. You may come across as too "sales-oriented," "phony," or just appear to be trying too hard.

Instead...

## Wear Clothing That:

- Is clean and ironed.

    This may be obvious, but check your clothes for spots, tears and wrinkles before you leave for your interview. You don't want to look messy and have your appearance recorded for eternity.

    And it's always a good idea to take a second, interview outfit with you in case you have a spill or if the producers do not like your original choice.

- Fits.

    Avoid wearing clothes that are too tight or too big. With tight clothing, viewers will not focus on what you have to say. With clothing that is too big, you will look larger on camera. Try to wear something that is tailored to your size and still looks neat when you sit down.

- Matches the style and tone of the program.

    If you are going to be on a casual talk-show, watch the program and see what the guests are wearing. Would it look strange to wear a suit on this show? Are all of the guests wearing more casual, business attire?

- Works with the interview activity.

    Think about what you are going to be doing on the program. Is it a sit-down interview, or will you be standing? Will you be outside or inside a studio? Also, will you be helping the host with a particular activity or demonstrating something?

    If you are going to be moving around, you need to take this into consideration. You want your clothes to look professional and stay in place so you are not fidgeting with a shirt, shoelace or other, clothing element.

- Includes solid colors.

    Usually, a solid, pale-colored shirt with a dark, solid-colored, suit jacket or sweater over it looks neat and professional on camera.

    Now, if you feel confident or lucky in a certain color, see if you can include it as part of your overall outfit. If you are supporting a specific business, sports team or charity, you may want to wear something that matches the logos or colors of these specific groups.

- Makes you feel good.

    Try to put on an outfit that makes you feel confident. Think about the colors and textures that you feel comfortable wearing and project the image you want to project.

    For example, if you are extremely tall or short and will feel uncomfortable standing next to the show's host, think about the shoes you'll be wearing. A little higher or lower heel may make you that much more confident and give you one less thing to worry about.

    And if you have a favorite color that gives you confidence, by all means, try to find an outfit that works with this color.

## Don't Sweat It.

This may seem like a lot of information, but you'll get the hang of it. And if you're really having trouble deciding, the best way to pick out the perfect outfit is to do a practice interview on camera prior to the real interview.

Not only will this help you practice what you are going to say, but you'll also get a better understanding of what you'll look like when you are saying it.

Also, start looking at your wardrobe *now*. If you don't have the right outfit, go shopping so you can find the perfect ensemble... on sale. And I highly suggest that you have two, different interview outfits ready to go at all times.

After all, you don't want to search for something to wear when you get a big interview at the last minute – or end up paying full price!

Instead, it's much better if you can stay calm and spend this valuable time reviewing the show and practicing your key talking-points.

## WHAT TO TAKE WITH YOU TO THE INTERVIEW

Once you secure an interview-date, lay out everything you need to wear the day before. You don't want to be rushing around finding and ironing clothes the morning of the interview. And last-minute emergencies can always come up that can take away from your precious prep-time.

Also, confirm the address and interview time with the producer the day before.

To make things easy for you, here is a simple checklist:

## Interview Checklist

| Item | Check |
|---|---|
| Media kit (3 Copies) | |
| Business cards | |
| Directions and map to interview location | |
| Cell phone (Be sure to turn it off when you arrive at the studio.) | |
| Any pertinent, product samples for host and producers (and to give away on the program) | |
| Extra shirt or blouse (It's a good idea to have a complete, second outfit ready to go in the car in case you spill something on your current outfit or the producer needs you to change.) | |
| Toothbrush, toothpaste, floss, and a mirror (Remember to check your teeth for food prior to your interview.) | |
| Bottle of water | |
| Ladies: face powder, hairspray, brush/comb, extra make-up, and any additional hair accessories | |
| Men: comb or brush, extra tie or hat (when appropriate) | |

If you're traveling a long distance to your interview, you'll want to create a separate list that includes all of the items you need to pack, what to wear on the way there and what to place in your "carry-on" bag.

And if you are traveling to the interview on an airplane, I highly suggest that you wear an appropriate interview-outfit or carry it on the aircraft with you. This way, if your luggage is lost, you'll still be prepared and save yourself a lot of anxiety.

Now, obviously this is a generic list. You'll need to update it pertinent to your specific needs and goals. And besides reviewing your talking points, you'll also want to check with your publicist to see if you need to take any specific items with you.

By having a list, you will know that you have everything you need. This will allow you to relax and focus on what you are going to say and do during the interview.

## AFTER THE INTERVIEW

**Move On.**

Great! You have completed your interview and are waiting patiently for it to air or be published. But please note, after you send out a press release, pitch a reporter or do an interview, I find it's always best not to get too excited about a potential media-placement until it actually happens.

*You may be very excited about your interview, but it is wise not to promote your upcoming story until it is actually published or broadcast.*

You can avoid a lot of heartache by waiting to celebrate a media interview until you actually see it in print, read it on the Internet, watch it on television, or hear it on the radio.

Why? Due to last-minute news, spacing, advertising placements, and numerous, other issues out of your control, stories are dropped all the time.

And even if your interview goes live, you have no idea how you and your organization will be portrayed in the story until you actually see it.

With this in mind, you'll save yourself a lot of embarrassment and energy if you have a little patience and understand that a completed interview doesn't necessarily mean a big, positive media-placement.

To deal with this situation, I highly suggest that you note the date the interview is scheduled to appear. Then, regularly monitor mentions of your name or company name online using a tool like Google® Alerts, www.google.com/alerts. And try not to publicize an upcoming, potential story until you see it live.

While you're waiting, move on to the other, public-relations activities in your PR Plan. For example, you can:

- Update your site.

When was the last time you updated your Web site with new content about your business? If you have news about employees, new partnerships, fresh products and services, or events, add this information to your site. After all, you want to appear "current" to the media and site visitors (more on this in a little while).

- Network.

Get out and meet people at local, business meetings, organizations and charity events in your area. While you're there, tell people what you do and how you help others with your products and services. This way, you can meet potential customers and build your referral network at the same time.

- <u>Present Valuable Information</u>.

Conduct research and find events occurring in your local area that focus on your target market. Then, volunteer to give a presentation at an upcoming meeting.

Provide valuable information and offer handouts of your products and services. Be entertaining without focusing on sales.

This allows you to build credibility as an expert in your field in front of your target market. Plus, you can promote the event, and get some potential, press coverage by local media-members.

- <u>Distribute News.</u>

Write and distribute at least one, SEO press release about your business once a month. Announce a speaking event or company news, comment on a current, industry trend, create and provide survey results, or provide some other, newsworthy information. Add the press release to your online newsroom, and mention it in your newsletters and correspondence.

This will remind your target market, and media-members, that your business is active and current. Plus, it's a cost-effective way to stay near the top of the search engines so that people can find you online when searching through news related to your industry.

- <u>Be Creative.</u>

While you communicate with team members and custom-ers, be aware of interesting success-stories, a significant increase in site visitors, major savings, and other, interesting data and changes within your organization.

You can use this kind of information to create new, press releases and media pitches that can lead to some major publicity. Your business has some valuable and unique news. You just need to look for good stories or create newsworthy activities on a regular basis.

These are just a few ideas to add to your PR Plan. But instead of focusing on one, pending media-placement that is supposed to appear in the next few weeks, continue working on a variety of PR activities pertinent to your overall goals.

This way, you'll build awareness, sales and credibility at a steady pace. And think how nice it will be when you open that major publication and are surprised to see your interview from weeks earlier!

## WHAT TO DO ONCE THE INTERVIEW GOES LIVE

### Review.

Finally, your business name appears in large letters in one of your targeted media-venues! Yay! Now what?

First, review the story carefully to see how you were quoted. If it was a recorded interview, look and listen for things you can improve on during your next interview.

Again, check to see if you said "Um" frequently, moved your head and arms too much, failed to promote the right marketing message, or made other mistakes. Remember. The more you review previous interviews and make appropriate adjustments, the faster your skills will improve.

And take heart. Not everyone has natural, interview and speaking skills. For many, it takes a lot of practice and experience to have a great interview every time.

Plus, you will deal with many kinds of reporters. Some will be friendly and easy to talk to. Others will probe for inside details and confidential information.

In the future, you'll know where you need improvements and to take more time to prepare, practice and review.

Eventually, you'll have more confidence and be able to handle all of your interview opportunities with ease. And it will be well worth the effort as your company reaps the benefits of the power of the press!

## WHO DO YOU TELL ABOUT YOUR MEDIA CLIP?

Obviously, you'll feel like telling everyone you know about your big media-clip when it appears. And that's not a bad idea. But you can organize the process so that you spread the news, and acquire as many benefits as possible from the media clip.

Here is a list of things to do once your media clip goes live:

- Send a thank you to the reporter.

    If possible, write a note to the reporter, producer or editor thanking him or her for the interview, and put it in the mail. This will show that you really appreciate their effort. If you are short on time, be sure to send an e-mail thank-you instead.

- Get permission to use the interview.

    Most media venues will allow you to link to the interview on their Web site. However, if you want to post the entire interview on your site, you will need to get permission and find out about copyright issues.

To get more information, contact the reporter, writer or producer you worked with or the venue's advertising department. And note that it's best to get approval in writing to avoid legal issues later on.

- Add the quote to your Web site.

    While you are getting approvals, it's o.k. to post a link to the media clip on your Web site newsroom and other pages. Just be sure to give full credit to the media venue.

    For example, on your newsroom, you could write a link like this:

    *2-17-10 – BtoB Online, "PrintingForLess taps into testimonials" by Nathan Gannon*

- Mention it in your blog and newsletter.

    Add a link to the article in your blog, newsletter and other, online marketing-materials. Also, post a link to the article via all of your social media venues such as Facebook, Twitter, LinkedIn, etc.

- Send a special note to potential investors, partners, etc.

    If the story gives your business credibility, be sure to send it to people you are trying to impress with a personal note. You don't want to sound egotistical, but you do want to spread the news.

    For example, you could say something like this at the end of an e-mail:

    "Have you seen our recent quote in BtoB at http://www. btobonline.com/apps/pbcs.dll/article?AID=/20100217/ FREE/100219935/1427/FREE?

We are thrilled to be able to share our tips and information with other entrepreneurs dealing with e-commerce issues."

- Add it to your media kit.

  Once you receive permission, be sure to add the new quote to your online and print media-kit. You may want to print several copies to send out with your next marketing-package too.

These are just a few of the things you can do with your media clip. In addition to these traditional methods, think of creative ways to spread the news.

*How can you use this quote to bring in new business and generate more buzz?*

- Perhaps you can frame it and post it in your front lobby for customers to see?

- Maybe your sales team can use it to impress potential clients and investors?

- And if other media-members aren't contacting you about this particular clipping, perhaps you can use it to entice a reporter on your target list to write about your business?

After all, you worked hard to obtain this placement so try to get the most out of it that you possibly can. And as you do subsequent interviews, you'll want to promote these clippings in the same way.

## NOT GETTING MEDIA CALLS?

Now, all of this interview information sounds great, but at this point, you may be frustrated.

If you're not receiving media calls and you've spent the appropriate time researching various venues, preparing your media kit, updating your online newsroom, and pitching reporters accordingly, there may be one key factor you've overlooked...

*Are you available?*

Many media-members work on very tight deadlines and need information immediately. If you are not available to answer questions, set interviews with company leaders or provide information, you will not get the media coverage you've worked so hard to obtain.

And please don't think reporters will just leave a message. If your phone keeps ringing or voicemail picks up, most reporters on deadline will immediately move on to another source.

As a small business owner, I know it can be very difficult to be available at all times. With this in mind, be sure to check your phone and e-mails frequently.

Another option is to have an assistant handle media requests for you. Just be sure to train this person accordingly, or you may miss out on some valuable, press opportunities.

For example, your assistant will need to find out the reporter, editor or producer's name, what media venue he or she is with and the deadline for the story. Then, your assistant should let you know about the call as soon as possible so you can respond immediately.

All media calls should get top priority. After all, one media mention can mean thousands of dollars in free publicity. Plus, you can start a relationship with a reporter that can result in many, additional media quotes in the future.

Yes, it's difficult to be available at all times. But by taking a few simple steps to provide reporters with the information they need, when they need it, you will have more media-placement opportunities.

More importantly, you will set your reputation as a professional who returns calls quickly, provides valuable information and is available to give reporters necessary data to meet tight deadlines.

## Don't Worry. There's Still Hope!

Ok. You've done your research, prepared appropriate press releases, created an online newsroom, and contacted reporters directly. But you are still not generating any buzz.

Well, as a small business owner, you probably know the importance persistence plays in obtaining key investors, partners and customers. This is true for your public-relations efforts too... so please don't get frustrated.

*Instead, work harder and review your activities.*

Timing is also an important factor. While some entrepreneurs get through to the press immediately, your efforts may not show results right away.

But if you consistently provide valuable information and wait for the right moment to contact specific media-members, you'll start to form relationships that will lead to future, press mentions.

With this in mind, here is a quick, reminder list to help you make the most of your persistent, PR efforts.

## PITCHING REMINDER-LIST

1. **Research before pitching.**

   As mentioned previously, it's essential to use targeted, marketing tactics to win new customers and grow your business. The same idea applies to working with the media.

   Before calling reporters or sending out press releases, it's essential to develop a unique, story angle for each media-member. By conducting the appropriate research, you'll have a better understanding of appropriate subject matter, deadlines and editorial calendars, and be able to pitch the right people at the right time.

2. **Follow up regularly.**

   After pitching your ideas to media-members, try to follow up. Reporters, producers and writers are swamped with deadlines, interviews and phone calls and can easily forget your most recent conversation.

   Be sure to call or e-mail the person you spoke with on a regular basis without being annoying. Keep in touch.

   It may take weeks, months or even years before your story fits into that media-member's schedule, but at least he or she will remember who you are and what you have to offer when the time is right.

3. **Hang in there.**

   Being persistent is important to public-relations success. Not only do you need to keep in touch with media-members on a regular basis with pertinent story ideas and pitches, but it is essential to keep going when a planned media-clipping falls through.

After all, there are many press opportunities available each month. It's up to you to find them and be ready to take action when the time is right!

# CHAPTER 7

# Build Buzz!

## MORE WAYS TO GENERATE PRESS

Now that you've started your initial, public-relations efforts, there are many ways to generate press, increase brand awareness and sales. Here are a few ideas and reminders:

**Update Your Copy.**

When potential, new customers and media-members visit your site, what do they see? Remember, your site should include current, up-to-date information about your products, services, news, and events.

If your site hasn't been updated lately, add appropriate copy so that site visitors, and the media, know that you are aware of industry trends and news and that your company is active. When your site is current, you convey a feeling of credibility and expertise. Plus, you'll significantly increase site traffic.

And the good news is that you don't need to spend a lot of money to update your Web site. To boost traffic and sales fast, try these cost-effective tips:

## 21 WAYS TO BOOST SITE TRAFFIC NOW

1. **Set specific business goals for your Web site.**

   Start fresh and review your site. Does it provide valuable and unique information to visitors, dramatically increase sales and new customers, or offer important benefits?

   You'll meet business goals faster if your Web site has a specific purpose. Decide what you want your Web site to do and concentrate on that specific result.

   Then, check to see if all of your content, photos and links focus on obtaining your goal, and make changes as necessary.

2. **Place important information on the first screen.**

   Does your logo take up a lot of space on the first screen of your Web site? If so, significantly reduce it and place it in the top, left-hand corner. This is where visitors are accustomed to seeing a logo.

   Then, use this valuable, site real-estate to highlight valuable benefits you have to offer. After all, site visitors want to know what you can do for them... not look at your logo.

3. **Stress benefits right away.**

   You have mere seconds to impress site visitors so let them know they are in the right place immediately. Focus on benefits and how you can help customers solve their problems.

And place this information in user-friendly, short copy on the top, middle portion of your site... where visitors tend to look first.

## 4. Talk to your customers.

Do you use a lot of big words and "corporate speak" on your site? If so, take time for customer research. Discover their likes and dislikes, popular trends and issues. Also look at competitors' sites.

The more you know about your customers, the better you will be able to connect with them on an emotional level with the right writing-style and tone.

## 5. Use emotion.

Since most people buy products and services based on emotion, your copy should reflect the specific desires of your customers.

Based on your research, help customers solve their unique problems quickly and easily. Relate to them on a personal level. And try to provide answers with honesty and integrity.

## 6. Replace passive verbs.

This is an easy tip that can make a huge difference...

*Is your online copy written in the present tense, or are you talking about things that happened in the past?*

You can instantly add energy to your site by replacing all of your past-tense verbs (we *worked* with this client, we *helped* XYZ when they *needed* to raise funds, etc.) with verbs that describe a current action (get help now, take advantage of our 25% discount today, boost sales fast, etc.).

7. **Keep it simple.**

To avoid customer confusion, focus on a single message per Web site page. It will be much easier to communicate clear and specific information to site visitors if you write about one topic per page.

8. **Write great headlines.**

Do your headlines convey positive, useful and specific information to help readers easily move through your Web site? Be sure to write brief headlines that offer unique benefits specific to your customers' needs.

9. **Add subheads.**

Since many visitors will simply scan your Web site, try to include mini-headlines that provide value. Just by reading your headlines and sub-headlines, potential customers should know what you have to offer, how you can help them and why they should use your products and services.

10. **Include bullet-points.**

Try to include user-friendly, bullet-points related to your key message for each Web site page. This gives site visitors easy-to-read benefits and unique information about your offerings at a glance.

11. **Keep sentences and paragraphs short.**

To keep readers interested, write short sentences and remove unnecessary adjectives, adverbs and other "fluff." Get to the point with your message and keep the momentum going.

## 12. Write what is necessary to make the sale.

While it is important to keep paragraphs and sentences short, you also need to write as much as necessary to sell your products and services. Usually, the more expensive the item you are selling, the more copy you need to sell it.

## 13. Be specific.

Whenever possible, try to provide specific information in your copy. This will add clarity and credibility.

For example, don't say, "We provide hundreds of widgets to charity each year." Say, "We provide 450 widgets to The Salvation Army®, The Pediatric Aids Foundation®, and Goodwill® each year."

## 14. Use photos that support your message.

The photos on your Web site should have a specific meaning and support your marketing message on each Web site page. If they don't help clarify your message, or provide an additional benefit, replace them with appropriate photos or delete them.

Also, where are you posting your photos? If the photos detract from your sales message, move them to the right side of your screen or to a Web site page specifically for photos.

## 15. Add captions to photos that are benefits.

Photo captions are read frequently by site visitors. Plus, many search engines pick up these brief statements. Use them to your advantage, and include a caption that stresses a benefit for each photo on your site.

## 16. Reprint testimonials.

To instantly improve credibility for your products and services, provide customer testimonials whenever possible. Try to obtain testimonials on a regular basis that include specific benefits and problems solved. And if the person is willing to give his or her name, business name, city, state, etc., this will increase the credibility of the testimonial.

Also, use testimonials "as is." They will sound more realistic if they are written in the voice of the customer – misspellings, bad grammar and all!

## 17. Have a call-to-action.

When potential customers take the time to read your Web site copy, do they know what to do in order to contact you or make a purchase?

Each page should have a specific and easy call-to-action. Whether it's registering for your newsletter, calling your sales department or actually purchasing a product online, be sure that Web site visitors know what they need to do.

## 18. Give a guarantee.

Try to remove all the doubts site visitors may have about purchasing your products and services. Provide a solid, user-friendly guarantee... and be sure to back it up with integrity.

Also include references whenever possible from current clients, industry associations and trusted organizations like the Better Business Bureau®.

### 19. Add a social-media component.

To build buzz, make it easy for site visitors to share your information with others. Add "Tell-A-Friend" buttons on every page of your site. Also, add simple links to shared media sources like Twitter, Facebook, MySpace®, www.myspace.com, etc.

### 20. Provide security.

Let customers know that their order will be private and safe. Include appropriate security information and pertinent seals from McAfee® PayPal®, Verisign®, or others.

### 21. Test.

Once you update your site, test variations on the copy, and use what works best to increase site visitors and the number of visitors who become buyers (conversion rates).

On a regular basis, use an appropriate, software program to test different words, photos, copy placements and more. At the time of this publishing date, Google Analytics offers a comprehensive service at no charge. By making a few changes, you can significantly boost sales.

## OPTIMIZE YOUR SITE.

If people search for your products and services via Google, Yahoo! or other search engines, will your business name appear in the results?

If not, you are missing out on thousands of potential, new customers, and it's time to add important keywords and coding to your overall site! But don't worry. As mentioned previously, the technical aspects of SEO are pretty simple, and you can do it yourself.

Here are a few tips to help you get started and optimize your site for the search engines:

### Research.

<u>Site Research</u>

To begin, conduct some research. Pretend you are one of your potential customers, and think about the words you would use to find your products and services online. Then, type these words into the various search engines like www.google.com, www.yahoo.com and www.msn.com.

*What sites appear first?*

Next, click on the sites at the top of the list. Once there, click on your right mouse button and then click on "View Source." You'll see all of the coding for that particular site.

For example, you may see some coding that looks like this:

<title>The site for unique flower baskets, exotic fruits and candies from all over the world</title>

<meta name="description" content="Unique flower baskets, exotic fruits and candies for the special person on your gift list. Call us for more information."/>

<meta name="keywords" content="flower baskets, exotic fruits, candy, gifts, unique gifts"/>

Now, you can see inside the site to see what keywords are listed. And you can also pull up your competitors' Web sites to see what words they are using too.

Make notes about the keywords in use on the various sites.

## Keyword-Tools Research

Once you do your own research, and think like your customers conducting a search, now it's time to use a keyword-search-tool to find the most popular, search terms and what will work best for you.

As mentioned previously, check out the free tools at www.keyworddiscovery.com/search.html and http://freekeywords.wordtracker.com/. Enter some keywords, and see what phrases and words come up. Then, create a list of your top words.

When you have your list of keywords compiled, pick your top choices and decide which words you'll focus on for each page of your Web site.

While you will overlap keywords on each page of your site, you will need to focus on three to four keyword phrases for each page.

### *Very Simple Coding-Tips*

Once you decide which keywords and phrases to use, you can insert them into the code of your site. Look at the examples you pulled up online and simply fill in the blanks:

### **Titles**

First, enter a different title for each page. Here, you want to provide strong content that reads like a headline and compels people to visit your site. As a guide, try to keep your total character count between 50 and 75 characters.

Sample:

<title>Your phrase here using your keywords</title>

### **Content Keywords**

Next, enter keywords that describe your business. These are the words that many search engines use when they pull up information about your site.

But please stick to five to seven keywords per page. If you try to place too many words in your coding, your efforts may backfire and the search engines may list your site as spam.

Sample:

<meta name="description" content="Insert a description of your site here. Search engines will often use this description when they find and post information about your site."/>

<meta name="keywords" content="gardening, colorful flower pots, garden tools, potting soil"/>

### Photo Tags

If site visitors are unable to see the photos on your site, alternative text will appear. In order to have some control over this situation, add "Alt tags" to each of your photos in the coding for your site. Place the code right after the coding for your photo.

Sample:

alt="Gardening tools to help you save time watering your flowers."

Now, these are just some very simple coding-tips you can apply to your site right away. It's best to continue your SEO education on a regular basis. Look online for free information and current updates. And as your business grows, you may want to outsource this function to a skilled and experienced, SEO professional.

## NETWORK.

Again, let me stress the importance of networking to your overall, business success. Try to attend pertinent, club meetings, events and presentations in your local area. Tell people about your products and services, and share your passion for your business.

Volunteer to speak about your industry at various organizations. Not only will you get in front of your target audience, but you may be quoted as a speaker in a local paper.

Remember, reporters usually cover important, community events so if you are a part of the activities, you significantly increase your chances of getting some free publicity. And even if press members do not attend, you will build some valuable business-relationships in this networking process.

## Distribute Press Releases.

Post press releases and announcements on a monthly basis with your current, contact information. This will help to remind key audiences and media-members that you are still doing business and have great news, information and success stories to tell.

Make it as easy as possible for media-members to know the products, services and expertise you have to offer. And provide current contact information so that they know how to get in touch with you at deadline time.

## Keep Your Eyes Open.

As things progress, look for good, customer case-studies, business innovations, financial and employee growth stories, and unique information that you can turn into a new story, event or announcement.

### Be Creative.

Some entrepreneurs have generated significant media attention by creating unique story-ideas, contests, surveys, gimmicks, splashy events, and more. By knowing your target audience and current news and industry trends, you'll have a better understanding of what will instigate "buzz" or word-of-mouth.

You can use public-relations activities to significantly build credibility and increase sales for your new business without spending a lot of money.

In fact, many new business owners have feature stories written about them after making just a few phone calls and pitching a great story. But note that this doesn't always happen so please don't get discouraged if you don't see results right away. More often, it takes persistence and time to build brand awareness and create media relationships.

*Remember, good publicity results from a lot of research and planning.*

But once you set goals for yourself, and follow through with an action-plan, appropriate written materials, targeted story-pitches, and creative events and ideas, you will see results.


## HIRING A PUBLICIST

Many entrepreneurs ask me how to get started with their PR efforts. And the most common questions pertain to finding a good publicist (because many, small business owners just don't have the time to do their own PR).

Before hiring a new public-relations expert or firm, it is essential to get as much information as possible. Research, review credentials, get references, and ask important questions.

To start, review your goals.

- What do you expect the publicist to do for your small business?

- What kind of budget do you have to work with?

- What are your immediate deadlines?

You really need to know exactly what you are expecting before speaking to a potential publicist. This way, you'll be able to clearly communicate your expectations and goals during your search.

When you are ready to interview a new, PR expert, here are some sample interview questions to ask:

## *Want to Hire a Publicist? Top 10 Questions To Ask!*

1. How many small businesses do you work with?

2. Do you work on a project-basis or by monthly/annual retainer? (Get contract details.)

3. What services are included in your fees and what is extra?

4. Who will be handling my account? (You, an intern, a team of people? Find out experience-levels of the people who will actually be working on your account.)

5. How will I know what is going on with my account? (Ask about communication methods and frequency.)

6. When will I see results?

7. Why should I use your services instead of going to someone else?

8. Can I try out your services first before making a long-term commitment?

9. What happens if I am not satisfied with your services?

10. Do you have references I can contact now?

These are just a few questions to keep in mind, and you'll want to add more that are pertinent to your specific needs. For additional help and information about the hiring process, contact the Public Relations Society of America, www.prsa.org.

And as a side note, be wary of anyone who can guarantee media-placements. In today's media world, full of last-minute news coverage and uncontrollable edits, it is very difficult to guarantee a publicity placement.

Also, look for someone that you feel comfortable with and can act as an extension of your team. And for your protection, be sure to sign a contract that both parties agree upon.

Publicity is a valuable tool to help build awareness and grow your business fast. But if you don't want to do it yourself, be sure to take the time to find the right publicist for your specific budget, goals and needs.

Otherwise, you might waste a lot money and effort without getting the results you want. And with this final note, it's time to...

## GO FOR IT!

Congratulations! Now you have a good foundation for pursuing your own PR activities and using the "power of the press" to grow your business.

And while all of this information may seem overwhelming at first, obtaining good publicity does not need to be difficult.

Just follow the simple steps in this book. And with a little research, practice and persistence, soon you'll be enjoying the business success that comes from a good, publicity program.

I wish you all the best!

# Additional Help

For additional assistance with your publicity efforts, updates and resources, please visit www.rembrandtwrites.com. Here, you'll find free reports, articles, blog entries, and more.

And don't forget to register for your *"Rembrandt Writes Insights®"* monthly newsletter. It's packed with valuable information to help you reach your goals.

If you have questions or need help with your PR and SEO copywriting activities, feel free to contact the author at:

Rembrandt Communications®
800 S. Pacific Coast Highway, Ste. #8-280
Redondo Beach, CA 90277
info@rembrandtwrites.com
www.rembrandtwrites.com

# About The Author

Melanie Rembrandt is one of the country's top, small business, public relations experts and the founder of Rembrandt Communications®, LLC. As a SEO copywriter, PR consultant with 20-plus years of extensive experience, an award-winning writer with hundreds of published works to her credit, and the author of "*Secrets of Becoming a Publicist,*" Melanie has an excellent, track record for helping entrepreneurs get the targeted, national media attention they need to boost sales, awareness and credibility fast.

A magna cum laude graduate of the prestigious UCLA School of Theater, Film and Television, Melanie is the PR expert for *StartupNation*®, *SmallBiz America*™ and *PINK Magazine*®. She also provides training presentations to organizations nationwide and valuable tips and information via her products, services and newsletter at www.rembrandtwrites.com

When not working, you can usually find Melanie teaching dance or several feet underwater scuba diving!

For more information and help taking your small business to the next level of success, visit www.rembrandtwrites.com.

Questions and comments about *"Simple Publicity"* may be sent to:

Rembrandt Communications®
800 S. Pacific Coast Highway, Ste. #8-280
Redondo Beach, CA 90277
info@rembrandtwrites.com
www.rembrandtwrites.com

LaVergne, TN USA
28 November 2010
206580LV00005B/96/P